Law and Order
Police Encounters

Trans-action Books

Law and Order
Police Encounters

Edited by

MICHAEL LIPSKY

Trans- **action** Books

Published by
Aldine Publishing Company

The essays in this book originally appeared
in *Trans-* **action** Magazine

363.2
L66L
74171
April, 1971

Contents

Preface

However diverse their attitudes and interpretations may sometimes be, social scientists are now entering a period of shared realization that the United States—both at home and abroad—has entered a crucial period of transition. Indeed, the much burdened word "crisis" has now become a commonplace among black militants, Wall Street lawyers, housewives, and even professional politicians.

For the past seven years, *Trans*-action magazine has dedicated itself to the task of reporting the strains and conflicts within the American system. But the magazine has done more than this. It has pioneered in social programs for changing the society, offered the kind of analysis that has permanently restructured the terms of the "dialogue" between peoples and publics, and offered the sort of prognosis that makes for real alterations in social and political policies directly affecting our lives.

The work done in the pages of *Trans*-action has crossed

professional boundaries. This represents much more than simple cross-disciplinary "team efforts." It embodies rather a recognition that the social world cannot be easily carved into neat academic areas. That, indeed, the study of the experience of blacks in American ghettos, or the manifold uses and abuses of agencies of law enforcement, or the sorts of overseas policies that lead to the celebration of some dictatorships and the condemnation of others, can best be examined from many viewpoints and from the vantage points of many disciplines.

This series of books clearly demonstrates the superiority of starting with real world problems and searching out practical solutions, over the zealous guardianship of professional boundaries. Indeed, it is precisely this approach that has elicited enthusiastic support from leading American social scientists for this new and dynamic series of books.

The demands upon scholarship and scientific judgment are particularly stringent, for no one has been untouched by the current situation. Each essay republished in these volumes bears the imprint of the author's attempt to communicate his own experience of the crisis. Yet, despite the sense of urgency these papers exhibit, the editors feel that many have withstood the test of time, and match in durable interest the best of available social science literature. This collection of *Trans*-action articles, then, attempts to address itself to immediate issues without violating the basic insights derived from the classical literature in the various fields of social science.

The subject matter of these books concern social changes that have aroused the long-standing needs and present-day anxieties of us all. These changes are in organizational life styles, concepts of human ability and intelligence, changing patterns of norms and morals, the relationship of social conditions to physical and biological environments, and in the status of social science with national policy making.

The dissident minorities, massive shifts in norms of social conduct, population explosions and urban expansions, and vast realignments between nations of the world of recent years do not promise to disappear in the seventies. But the social scientists involved as editors and authors of this *Trans*-action series have gone beyond observation of these critical areas, and have entered into the vital and difficult tasks of explanation and interpretation. They have defined issues in a way making solutions possible. They have provided answers as well as asked the right questions. Thus, this series should be conceived as the first collection dedicated not to hightlighting social problems alone, but to establishing guidelines for social solutions based on the social sciences.

THE EDITORS
Trans-action

Introduction

MICHAEL LIPSKY

The study of the ways police interact with other citizens is of primary importance for anyone concerned with public policy and the just resolution of contemporary urban conflict. Policemen may be conceived as "street-level bureaucrats" who "represent" government to people. And at the same time as they represent government policies, police forces also help define the terms of urban conflict by their actions. The influence of police on political attitudes and developments is fundamental because of the unique role of law enforcement agencies in enforcing and reinforcing the norms of the system.

Few readers of this book will be unfamiliar with the events described in the first two articles reprinted from the pages of *trans*-action. Forty-three persons were killed in the Detroit riot which erupted in the early hours of July 23, 1967. Racial violence in previous decades had been initiated by white mobs and carried out with the acquiescence of law enforcement personnel. But since the Watts rebellion of 1964, and continuing at least through the outbreaks following the murder of Martin Luther King, Jr., racial disorders have typically been precipitated by the police and have subsequently been characterized by black destruction of property and antagonism directed against the police.

The testimony of black Detroit residents taken by Tom Parmenter provides a perspective on racial disturbances often unavailable to white audiences. By talking to people in the midst of the riot, Parmenter is able to round out more systematic post facto explorations of black attitudes toward riots. The journalist's technique permits presentation of a witness's full perspective. Parmenter's account offers what is often smoothed over and neglected in attitudinal surveys: the rich ambivalence that participants and observers felt at the time. Moreover, he captures attitudes that are relatively free of the rationalizations that take over after the smoke has cleared and basic responses have been modified by communications media and public reconstruction of events. Parmenter can make no claim that his interviews are representative; but they are illuminating in particularly important ways.

If the black rebellions of the sixties may be appropriately characterized as property-directed, the Chicago police riot during the National Democratic Convention represented a return to group combat. The remarkable report by Attorney Daniel Walker prepared for the President's Commission on the Causes and Prevention of Violence (a portion of which is presented here) details the loss of control and the unrestrained, indiscriminate brutality exhibited by Chicago policemen on the night of August 28, 1968. The events of that night may have been a turning point in American politics, as Tom Wicker of the *New York Times* has suggested.

For many people the frightening issue of that night is not so much whether there was provocation from both sides—for surely there was—but what kind of behavior should be expected from law enforcement officials and to what extent police preparation provoked the confrontation. Under what circumstances may a well-trained, relatively modern police force lose control and deny fundamental liberties not only to antagonists, but, in the excitement of the moment, to anyone who happens to be nearby?

These questions cannot be answered authoritatively; indeed, social scientists have barely begun to ask the right questions about police behavior. The articles collected here do, however, present a series of critical issues which students of police behavior must confront.

To what extent does police behavior (as in other bureaucratic contexts) result from a structuring of events by the police organization itself? That the police may generate and create conditions for the realization of "self-fulfilling prophecies" is illustrated in these articles in a number of ways. For example, a black community organizer suggested to Tom Parmenter that police provoked the Detroit riots. "Overreaction" is the euphemism by which such responses are generally known in descriptions of police behavior during civil disorders. Similarly, both in the Detroit riot and in general accounts of sniping incidents, as Terry Ann Knopf argues in another article, police expectations of sniper activity may result in the kind of surveillance and response tactics that exacerbate conflict.

Another way in which police actions may result in creating the very behavior they are supposed to suppress is the police practice of identifying what Jerome Skolnick calls "potential assailants." Police commonly develop a "shorthand" by which they can more easily identify individuals with whom they anticipate difficulty. The shorthand may consist of generalizations about people with certain skin color, hair length or clothing style. Black people in America have always been discriminated against by police on the basis of this kind of simplification. Deviants may also evoke police hostility because of presumed characteristics, as Albert Reiss discovered in his investigation of police brutality. The simplifications employed by police, and the circumstances in which these simplifications are invoked, may result in increasing the number of the very antagonists which police manifestly attempt to minimize. One could argue that the police riot in Chicago in part occurred because police extended generalizations about potential assailants to everyone who looked like a "hippie," against whom they had been warned.

One way in which this kind of analysis can be employed is demonstrated in Robert Shellow and Derek Roemer's description of how the police handled a potentially explosive encounter with motorcyclists scheduled to inundate the seat of a Washington, D.C., suburban county. As tactical advisers to local police officials, Shellow and Roemer were able to help the police appreciate the distinction between provocative appearance and unlawful behavior. They were also able to help them distinguish among levels of provocative behavior, so as to avoid precipitating large-scale incidents because of concern for minor infractions. As described by these social scientists, the police successfully negotiated the weekend because of the intelligence on which they were able to act. (In recognition of this apparently successful integration of theory and practice, the editor, no great optimist himself, concludes the volume with this article.)

Albert Reiss' article on police brutality provides evidence for both sides of the debate concerning police brutality in

American cities. On the one hand, Reiss' research staff documented clear instances of police brutality, demonstrated that the average black citizen is more likely to be brutalized than his white counterpart, and showed that police brutality is predominantly a matter of police victimization of the lower classes, at least in the context studied. On the other hand, whether the rates are "high" or "low" may be a matter of personal judgment, preference and taste. Reiss indicates that his findings may be conservatively biased because of the intrusion of the research/observer. But whether they are "high" or "low," police brutality is certain to be seen differently by different segments of the population. Although more whites than blacks are brutalized in Reiss' observations, upper- and middle-class whites are effectively shielded from knowledge of police shortcomings by their economic and residential segregation. Almost all blacks thus are witness to brutality more often. Middle- and upper-class white populations have distinctly different impressions of police behavior from those of blacks, who, because of discrimination, for the most part are denied the "privilege" of segregating themselves along class lines. The Reiss study does not present figures on harassment, which might display different rates of hostile interactions between middle-class blacks and police. Be that as it may, the level of police brutality which will invoke feelings of hostility toward the police is a function of the particular circumstances in which groups live; rates are meaningless without such considerations.

The impact of segregated living on middle-class blacks, may also be inferred from the article by Philip Ennis. He shows that middle-class blacks are more likely to become victims of crimes against property than their white counterparts, and more likely to believe that policemen are corrupt than either their white counterparts or their less affluent brothers. Thus middle-class blacks are doubly alienated from the police: they are both more exposed to police brutality and more in need of police protection.

Philip Ennis also alerts the reader to the spongy nature of crime statistics. In a special sense it is fair to say that we have "crime waves" when people expect crime waves to exist. Crime "rates," like other figures generated in bureaucratic contexts, must always be recognized as imperfect indicators of reality. They may be biased or skewed in predictable directions, depending upon the methods of data collection and the needs and motivating factors of the collection agent. For instance, organizations may have a stake in rising rates (as do agencies whose budgets depend upon per capita financing) or in falling rates (as do agencies rewarded for minimizing the caseload). Heavier surveillance may result in higher crime rates, although the actual incidence of crime has not changed. Furthermore, formal or informal redefinition of offenses may result in rate changes without actually being accompanied by changes in behavior. Client expectations of the service they are likely to get may also significantly affect people's tendency to report crimes. This is suggested by Ennis' finding that except for homicides, car thefts are the only crimes that victims tend to report at the same rate as his statistics say they are robbed. People will report crimes when they believe that the positive benefits will be greater than the actual and psychological cost. Apparently, with many crimes, the anticipated costs are often greater than the expected benefits. But with car thefts, people seem to believe in the likelihood of successful police intervention; additionally, they need to report car theft for insurance purposes. Hence the relatively greater "accuracy" of the F.B.I.'s car theft statistics.

If crime rates are a product as well as a reflection of law enforcement agency practices, to what extent are other reports of police encounters with citizens also products of police creation? Terry Ann Knopf, in her analysis of sniping as an alleged new pattern of violence, suggests that while sniping may have occurred in some recent police encounters, the reported incidence of sniping has been grossly exaggerated by a confused constabulary and by newspaper people who are eager to report sensational developments and unable or unwilling to validate sniping reports independently because of pressures of daily deadlines. Miss Knopf's article suggests that a mythology of sniping has been developed which has alarmed the middle class out of proportion to the facts, and may have resulted in inspiring additional sniper activity.

Like the sister myth that urban riots are caused by the "riff-raff" of the ghetto, Americans appear to have accepted unquestioningly a view of ghetto riots and their participants that functions to shield them from the urgency of whatever political messages are being transmitted by people in revolt. To say that the current wave of ghetto unrest is dominated by sniping is not only an exaggeration, it may also serve to deflect attention away from legitimate political expressions by falsely attributing murderous tactics to a large segment of American society, well known for its patience in the past, whose relative patience may still be noted as of this writing.

Confrontation
at the Conrad Hilton

FROM THE WALKER COMMISSION REPORT
RIGHTS IN CONFLICT

A police riot. A reporter coined that phrase in attempting to capsulize the melee involving Chicago police and demonstrators in Chicago's Grant Park during the Democratic National Convention of August 1968. The words were immortalized by a Chicago study team on assignment from the President's Commission on the Causes and Prevention of Violence. The task of the study team was to find out what happened in Chicago and why. The result of its 53-day investigation was a documented report released December 1, 1968, entitled "Rights in Conflict," and bearing the name of a Chicago corporate attorney, Daniel Walker, who directed the investigation throughout and insisted on its immediate and unexpurgated publication despite pressure from some on the violence commission who wanted obscenity in the report toned down and publication delayed until at least next spring.

The report is based on 3,436 statements of eyewitnesses

9

and participants taken by the Walker committee and by the FBI. Those interviewed included police officers, National Guardsmen, United States Army personnel, demonstrators and their leaders, government officials, convention delegates, news media representatives and bystanders. The staff also viewed about 180 hours of motion picture film provided by television networks and local stations, the Chicago police department and others. More than 12,000 photographs were examined and official police and National Guard records were reviewed.

It is important to note that although individual members of Students for a Democratic Society, and other allied organizations linked to the National Mobilization Committee to End the War in Vietnam, were interviewed, the organizations themselves refused to cooperate with the study team. Thus, there is a likelihood in the report of considerable under-reporting of mass spontaneous violence.

Violence marked police-demonstrator relations from beginning to end of the convention, but none was so vicious as the bloody clash Wednesday evening, August 28, in front of the Conrad Hilton Hotel, where many delegates were staying and where the presidential campaign headquarters of Senator Eugene J. McCarthy was located. The following story is taken from the Walker Commission report. It is the step-by-step, indeed, nearly blow-by-blow account of events leading to the clash.

By about 5 p.m. Wednesday the U.S. Attorney's report says about 2000 persons, "mostly normally dressed," had already assembled at the [Conrad] Hilton [Hotel]. Many of these were demonstrators who had tired of waiting out the negotiations and had broken off from the marchers and made their way to the hotel. It appears that police al-

ready were having some difficulty keeping order at that location. Says the U.S. Attorney's report: "A large crowd had
assembled behind the police line along the east wall of the
Hilton. This crowd was heavily infiltrated with 'Yippie'
types and was spitting and screaming obscene insults at the
police."

A policeman on duty in front of the hotel later said that
it seemed to him that the obscene abuses shouted by "wom-
en hippies" outnumbered those called out by male demonstrators "four to one." A common epithet shouted by the
females, he said, was "Fuck you, pig." Others included
references to policemen as "cock suckers" and "mother
fuckers."

A short time later a reporter noticed a lot of debris being
hurled from one of the upper floors of the Hilton. He
climbed into a police squad car parked in the area and with
the aid of police binoculars saw that rolls of toilet paper
were coming from the 15th floor, a location he pinpointed
by counting down from the top of the building. He then
went to the 15th floor and found that the section the paper
was coming from was rented by Senator McCarthy cam-
paigners. He was not admitted to the suite.

If Dellinger's marchers in Grant Park now moved to the
Hilton area, an additional 5000 demonstrators would be
added to the number the police there would have to control.

At about 6 or 6:30 p.m., one of the march leaders announced by loudspeaker that the demonstrators would not
be allowed to march to the Amphitheatre. He told the
crowd to disperse and to re-group in front of the Conrad
Hilton Hotel in Grant Park.

Police in the area were in a far from cheerful mood. A
neatly dressed sociology student from Minnesota says he
stepped off the sidewalk onto the grass and two policemen
pulled their billy clubs back as though ready to swing. One
of them said, "You'd better get your fucking ass off that
grass or I'll put a beautiful goddam crease in your fucking

queer head." The student overheard another policeman say to a "hippie-looking girl of 14 or 15, 'You better get your fucking dirty cunt out of here.' " The growing feeling of entrapment was intensified and some witnesses noticed that police were letting people into the park but not out. The marshals referred to the situation as a "trap."

As the crowd moved north, an Assistant U.S. Attorney saw one demonstrator with long sideburns and hippie garb pause to break up a large piece of concrete, wrapping the pieces in a striped T-shirt.

Before the march formally disbanded, an early contingent of demonstrators, numbering about 30 to 50, arrived at the spot where Congress Plaza bridges the Illinois Central tracks at approximately the same time as a squad of 40 National Guardsmen. The Guard hurriedly spread out about three feet apart across Congress with rifles at the ready, gas masks on, bayonets fixed.

Now as the bulk of the disappointed marchers sought a way out of the park, the crowd began to build up in front of the Guard. "I saw one woman driving a new red late-model car approach the bridge," a news correspondent says: "Two demonstrators, apparently badly gassed, jumped into the back seat and hoped to get through the Guard lines. Guardsmen refused to permit the car through, going so far as to threaten to bayonet her tires and the hood of her car if she did not turn around. One Guardsman fired tear gas point blank beside the car."

The crowd's basic strategy, a medic recalled, was "to mass a sizeable group at one end of the line," as if preparing to charge. Then, when Guardsmen shifted to protect that area, a comparatively small group of demonstrators would push through the weak end of the line. Once the small group had penetrated the line, the medic says, members would "come up behind the Guardsmen and taunt them, as well as push and shove them from the rear." A Guard official said later that his men were attacked with oven cleaner and containers filled with excrement.

As the crowd swelled, it surged periodically towards the Guard line, sometimes yelling, "Freedom, freedom." On one of these surges a Guardsman hurled two tear gas canisters. Some of the tear gas was fired directly into the faces of demonstrators. "We came across a guy really badly gassed," a college coed says. "We were choking, but we could still see. But this guy we saw was standing there helpless with mucous-type stuff on his face, obviously in pain."

An Assistant U.S. Attorney says he saw "hundreds of people running, crying, coughing, vomiting, screaming." Some woman ran blindly to Buckingham Fountain and leaped into the water to bathe their faces. The Guard medic quoted earlier says he was again assaulted by demonstrators when he went into the crowd to treat a man felled by "a particularly heavy dose of tear gas."

"In Grant Park, the gassed crowd was angered . . . more aggressive," says the history professor. Shortly after the gassing, says the Guard medic quoted earlier, "two forces of police arrived. They immediately waded into the crowd with clubs swinging indiscriminately, driving them off the bridge and away from the area." Once more, the Guardsman said, he was assaulted by demonstrators—this time when he tried "to treat an individual who received a severe head injury from the police."

Surging north from Congress Plaza to a footbridge leading from the park, the crowd encountered more Guardsmen. More tear gas was dispensed. Surging north from the site of the gassings, the crowd found the Jackson Boulevard bridge unguarded. Word was quickly passed back by loudspeaker, "Two blocks north, there's an open bridge; no gas." As dusk was settling, hundreds poured from the park into Michigan Avenue.

At 7:14 p.m., as the first groups of demonstrators crossed the bridge toward Michigan Avenue, they noticed that the mule train of the Poor People's Campaign was just entering the intersection of Michigan and Jackson, headed south.

The wagons were painted, "Jobs & Food for All."

The train was accompanied by 24 policemen on foot, five on three-wheelers, and four in two squadrols. A police official was in front with the caravan's leaders. The sight of the train seemed to galvanize the disorganized Grant Park crowd and those streaming over the bridge broke into cheers and shouts. "Peace now!" bellowed the demonstrators. "Dump the Hump!" This unexpected enthusiastic horde in turn stimulated the mule train marchers. Drivers of the wagons stood and waved to the crowd, shouting: "Join us! Join us!" To a young man watching from the 23rd floor of the Hilton Hotel, "the caravan seemed like a magnet to demonstrators leaving the park."

When the crowd's first rank reached the intersection of Balbo and Michigan, the northeast corner of the Hilton, it was close to approximately 2000 to 3000 demonstrators and spectators. The police were armed with riot helmets, batons, mace, an aerosol tear gas can and their service revolvers (which they always carry). Behind the police lines, parked in front of the Hilton, was a fire department high pressure pumper truck hooked up to a hydrant. Pairs of uniformed firemen were also in the vicinity. The growing crowds, according to the U.S. Attorney's report, were a blend of "young and old, hippies, Yippies, straights, newsmen and cameramen," even two mobile TV units.

From within the crowd were rising the usual shouts from some of the demonstrators: "Hell no, we won't go!" . . . "Fuck these Nazis!" . . . "Fuck you, L.B.J.!" . . . "No more war!" . . . 'Pigs, pigs, pigs." . . . "The streets belong to the people!" . . . "Let's go to the Amphitheatre!" . . . "Move on, Move on!" . . . "You can't stop us." . . . "From the hotel," recalls a student, "people who sympathized were throwing confetti and pieces of paper out of the windows and they were blinking their room lights."

Occasionally during the early evening, groups of demonstrators would flank the police lines or find a soft spot and punch through, heading off on their own for the Amphitheatre. On the periphery of the Hilton and on thorough-fares and side streets further southwest, a series of brief but sometimes violent encounters occurred.

For example, says the manager of a private club on Michigan Avenue, "a large band of long-haired demonstrators . . . tore down the American flag" overhanging the entrance to the club "and took it into Michigan Avenue attempting to tear it."

At about 7 p.m. from the window of a motel room in the 1100 block of South Michigan, a senator's driver noticed a group of demonstrators walking south, chanting: "Hell no, we won't go!" and "Fuck the draft." They were hurling insults at passing pedestrians and when one answered back, the witness says, "five demonstrators charged out of Michigan Avenue onto the sidewalk, knocked the pedestrian down, formed a circle around his fallen body, locked their arms together and commenced kicking him in a vicious manner. When they had finished kicking their victim, they unlocked their arms and immediately melted back into the crowd. . . ."

Vice President Humphrey was now inside the Conrad Hilton Hotel and the police commanders were afraid that the crowd might either attempt to storm the hotel or march south on Michigan Avenue, ultimately to the Amphitheatre. The Secret Service had received an anonymous phone call that the Amphitheatre was to be blown up. A line of police was established at 8th and Michigan at the south end of the hotel and the squads of police stationed at the hotel doors began restricting access to those who could display room keys. Some hotel guests, including delegates and Senator McCarthy's wife, were turned away.

By 7:30 p.m. a rumor was passing around that the Black-stone Rangers and the East Side Disciples, two of Chicago's most troublesome street gangs, were on their way to the scene. (This was later proven to be untrue; neither of these South Side gangs was present in any numbers in either Lincoln Park or Grant Park.) At this point, a

Negro male was led through the police line by a police officer. He spoke to the police officer, a city official and a deputy superintendent of police. He told them that he was in charge of the mule train and that his people wanted no part of this mob. He said he had 80 people with him, that they included old people and children, and he wanted to get them out of the mob. The police officer later stated the group wanted to go past the Hilton, circle it, and return to the front of the hotel where Reverend Ralph Abernathy could address the crowd.

In a few minutes, Reverend Ralph Abernathy appeared and, according to the police officer's statement, "said he wanted to be taken out of the area as he feared for the safety of his group." The police officer directed that the train be moved south on Michigan to 11th Street and then, through a series of turns through the Loop, to the West Side.

A policeman on Michigan later said that at about this time a "female hippie" came up to him, pulled up her skirt and said, "You haven't had a piece in a long time." A policeman standing in front of the Hilton remembers seeing a blond female who was dressed in a short red minidress make lewd, sexual motion in front of a police line. Whenever this happened, he says, the policemen moved back to prevent any incident. The crowd, however, egged her on, the patrolman says. He thought that "she and the crowd wanted an arrest to create a riot." Earlier in the same general area a male youth had stripped bare and walked around carrying his clothes on a stick.

The intersection at Balbo and Michigan was in total chaos at this point. The street was filled with people. Darkness had fallen but the scene was lit by both police and television lights. As the mule train left, part of the group tried to follow the wagons through the police line and were stopped. According to the deputy superintendent of police, there was much pushing back and forth between the policemen and the demonstrators.

Continual announcements were made at this time over a police amplifier for the crowd to "clear the street and go up on the sidewalk or into the park area for their demonstrations." The broadcast said, "Please gather in the park on the east side of the street. You may have your peaceful demonstration and speechmaking there." The demonstrators were also advised that if they did not heed these orders they would face arrest. The response from many in the crowd, according to a police observer, was to scream and shout obscenities. A Chicago attorney who was watching the scene recalls that when the announcements were broadcast, "No one moved." The deputy superintendent then made another announcement: "Will any non-demonstrators, anyone who is not a part of this group, any newsmen, please leave the group." Despite the crowd noise, the loud-speaker announcements were "loud and plainly heard," according to an officer.

While this was happening on Michigan Avenue, a separate police line had begun to move east toward the the crowd from the block of Balbo that lies between Michigan and Wabash along the north side of the Hilton.

Just as the police in front of the Hilton were confronted with some sit-downs on the south side of the intersection of Balbo and Michigan, the police unit coming into the intersection on Balbo met the sitting demonstrators. What happened then is subject to dispute between the police and some other witnesses.

The Balbo police unit commander asserts that he informed the sit-downs and surrounding demonstrators that if they did not leave, they would be arrested. He repeated the order and was met with a chant of "Hell no, we won't go." Quickly a police van swung into the intersection immediately behind the police line, the officers opened the door at the rear of the wagon. The deputy chief "ordered the arrest process to start."

"Immediately upon giving this order," the deputy chief later informed his superiors, "we were pelted with rocks, bottles, cans filled with unknown liquids and other debris, which forced the officers to defend themselves from injury. . . . My communications officer was slugged from behind by one of these persons, receiving injuries to his right eye and cheekbone."

The many films and video tapes of this time period present a picture which does not correspond completely with the police view. First, the films do not show a mob moving west on Balbo; they show the street as rather clean of the demonstrators and bystanders, although the sidewalks themselves on both sides of the street are crowded. Second, they show the police walking east on Balbo, stopping in formation, awaiting the arrival of the van and starting to make arrests on order. A total of 25 seconds elapses between their coming to a halt and the first arrests.

Also, a St. Louis reporter who was watching from inside the Haymarket lounge agrees that the police began making arrests "in formation," apparently as "the result of an order to clear the intersection." Then, the reporter adds, "from this apparently controlled beginning the police began beating people indiscriminately. They grabbed and beat anyone they could get hold of."

"The crowd tried to reverse gears," the reporter says. "People began falling over each other. I was in the first rank between police and the crowd and was caught in the first surge. I went down as I tried to retreat. I covered my head, tried to protect my glasses which had fallen partially off, and hoped that I would not be clubbed. I tried to dig into the humanity that had fallen with me. You could hear shouting and screaming. As soon as I could, I scrambled to my feet and tried to move away from the police. I saw a youth running by me also trying to flee. A policeman clubbed him as he passed, but he kept running.

"The cops were saying, 'Move! I said, move, god dammit! Move, you bastards!'" A representative of the ACLU who was positioned among the demonstrators says the police "were cussing a lot" and were shouting, "Kill,

kill, kill, kill, kill!" A reporter for the *Chicago Daily News* said after the melee that he, too, heard this cry. A demonstrator remembers the police swinging their clubs and screaming, "Get the hell out of here." . . . "Get the fuck out of here." . . . "Move your fucking ass!"

The crowd frantically eddied in a halfmoon shape in an effort to escape the officers coming in from the west. A UPI reporter who was on the southern edge of the crowd on Michigan Avenue, said that the advancing police "began pushing the crowd south." A cherry bomb burst overhead. The demonstrators strained against the deputy superintendent of police's line south of the Balbo-Michigan intersection. "When I reached that line," says the UPI reporter, "I heard a voice from behind it say, 'Push them back, move them back!' I was then prodded and shoved with nightsticks back in a northerly direction, toward the still advancing line of police."

"Police were marching this way and that," a correspondent from a St. Louis paper says. "They obviously had instructions to clear the street, but apparently contradicting one another in the directions the crowd was supposed to be sent."

The deputy superintendent of police recalls that he ordered his men to "hold your line there" . . . "stand fast" . . . "Lieutenant, hold your men steady there!" These orders, he said, were not obeyed by all. He said that police disregarded his order to return to the police lines—the beginning of what he says was the only instance in which he personally saw police discipline collapse. He estimates that ten to 15 officers moved off on individual forays against demonstrators.

Thus, at 7:57 p.m., with two groups of club-wielding police converging simultaneously and independently, the battle was joined. The portions of the throng out of the immediate area of conflict largely stayed put and took up the chant, "The whole world is watching," but the intersection fragmented into a collage of violence.

Re-creating the precise chronology of the next few moments is impossible. But there is no question that a violent street battle ensued.

People ran for cover and were struck by police as they passed. Clubs were swung indiscriminately.

"I saw squadrons of policemen coming from everywhere," a secretary said. "The crowd around me suddenly began to run. Some of us, including myself, were pushed back onto the sidewalk and then all the way up against . . . the Blackstone Hotel along Michigan Avenue. I thought the crowd had panicked."

"Fearing that I would be crushed against the wall of the building . . . I somehow managed to work my way . . . to the edge of the street . . . and saw police everywhere.

"As I looked up I was hit for the first time on the head from behind by what must have been a billy club. I was then knocked down and while on my hands and knees, I was hit around the shoulders. I got up again, stumbling and was hit again. As I was falling, I heard words to the effect of 'move, move' and the horrible sound of cracking billy clubs.

"After my second fall, I remember being kicked in the back, and I looked up and noticed that many policemen around me had no badges on. The police kept hitting me on the head."

Eventually she made her way to an alley behind the Blackstone and finally, "bleeding badly from my head wound," was driven by a friend to a hospital emergency room. Her treatment included the placing of 12 stitches.

A lawyer says that he was in a group of demonstrators in the park just south of Balbo when he heard a police officer shout, "Let's get 'em!" Three policemen ran up, "singled out one girl and as she was running away from them, beat her on the back of the head. As she fell to the ground, she was struck by the nightsticks of these officers." A male friend of hers then came up yelling at the police. The witness said, "He was arrested. The girl was left in the area lying on the ground."

A *Milwaukee Journal* reporter says in his statement, "when the police managed to break up groups of protesters they pursued individuals and beat them with clubs. Some police pursued individual demonstrators as far as a block . . . and beat them. . . . In many cases it appeared to me that when police had finished beating the protesters they were pursuing, they then attacked, indiscriminately, any civilian who happened to be standing nearby. Many of these were not involved in the demonstrations."

In balance, there is no doubt that police discipline broke during the melee. The deputy superintendent of police states that—although this was the only time he saw discipline collapse—when he ordered his men to stand fast, some did not respond and began to sally through the crowd, clubbing people they came upon. An inspector-observer from the Los Angeles Police Department, stated that during this week, "The restraint of the police both as individual members and as an organization, was beyond reason." However, he said that on this occasion:

> *There is no question but that many officers acted without restraint and exerted force beyond that necessary under the circumstances. The leadership at the point of conflict did little to prevent such conduct and the direct control of officers by first-line supervisors was virtually non-existent.*

The deputy superintendent of police has been described by several observers as being very upset by individual policemen who beat demonstrators. He pulled his men off the demonstrators, shouting "Stop, damn it, stop. For Christ's sake, stop it."

"It seemed to me," an observer says, "that only a saint could have swallowed the vile remarks to the officers. However, they went to extremes in clubbing the Yippies. I saw them move into the park, swatting away with clubs at girls and boys lying in the grass. More than once I witnessed two officers pulling at the arms of a Yippie until the arms almost left their sockets, then, as the officers put the Yippie in a police van, a third jabbed a riot stick into the groin of the youth being arrested. It was evident that the Yippie was not resisting arrest."

"In one incident, a young man, who apparently had been maced, staggered across Michigan . . . helped by a companion. The man collapsed. . . . Medical people from the volunteer medical organization rushed out to help him. A police officer (a sergeant, I think) came rushing forward, followed by the two other nightstick-brandishing policemen and yelled, 'Get him out of here; this ain't a hospital.' The medical people fled, half dragging and half carrying the young man with them. . . ."

During the course of arrests, one girl lost her skirt. Although there have been unverified reports of police ripping the clothes from female demonstrators, this is the only incident on news film of any woman being disrobed in the course of arrest.

While violence was exploding in the street, the crowd wedged, behind the police sawhorses along the northeast edge of the Hilton, was experiencing a terror all its own. Early in the evening, this group had consisted in large part of curious bystanders. But following the police surges into the demonstrators clogging the intersection, protesters had crowded the ranks behind the horses in their flight from the police.

From force of numbers, this sidewalk crowd of 150 to 200 persons was pushing down toward the Hilton's front entrance. Policemen whose orders were to keep the entrance clear were pushing with sawhorses. Other police and fleeing demonstrators were pushed from the north in the effort to clear the intersection. Thus, the crowd was wedged against the hotel, with the hotel itself on the west, sawhorses on the southeast and police on the northeast.

Films show that one policeman elbowed his way to where he could rescue a girl of about ten years of age from the vise-like press of the crowd. He cradled her in his arms and carried her to a point of relative safety 20 feet away. The crowd itself "passed up" an elderly woman to a low ledge.

"I was crowded in with the group of screaming, frightened people," an onlooker states, "We jammed against each other, trying to press into the brick wall of the hotel. As we stood there breathing hard . . . a policeman calmly walked the length of the barricade with a can of chemical spray [evidently mace] in his hand. Unbelievably, he was spraying at us." Photos reveal several policemen using mace against the crowd. "Some of the police then turned and attacked the crowd," a Chicago reporter says. A young cook caught in the crowd relates that:

"The police began picking people off. They would pull individuals to the ground and begin beating them. A medic wearing a white coat and an armband with a red cross was grabbed, beaten and knocked to the ground. His whole face was covered with blood."

As a result, a part of the crowd was trapped in front of the Conrad Hilton and pressed hard against a big plate glass window of the Haymarket Lounge. A reporter who was sitting inside said, "Frightened men and women banged . . . against the window. A captain of the fire department inside told us to get back from the window, that it might get knocked in. As I backed away a few feet I could see a smudge of blood on the glass outside."

With a sickening crack, the window shattered, and screaming men and women tumbled through, some cut badly by jagged glass. The police came after them. "A patrolman ran up to where I was sitting," said a man with a cut leg. "I protested that I was injured and could not walk, attempting to show him my leg. He screamed that he would show me I could walk. He grabbed me by the shoulder and literally hurled me through the door of the bar into the lobby. . . .

"I stumbled out into what seemed to be a main lobby.

The young lady I was with and I were both immediately set upon by what I can only presume were plainclothes police. . . . We were cursed by these individuals and thrown through another door into an outer lobby." Eventually a McCarthy aide took him to the 15th floor.

In the heat of all this, probably few were aware of the Haymarket's advertising slogan: "A place where good guys take good girls to dine in the lusty, rollicking atmosphere of fabulous Old Chicago. . . ."

There is little doubt that during this whole period, beginning at 7:57 p.m. and lasting for nearly 20 minutes, the preponderance of violence came from the police. It was not entirely a one-way battle, however.

Firecrackers were thrown at police. Trash baskets were set on fire and rolled and thrown at them. In one case, a gun was taken from a policeman by a demonstrator.

"Some hippies," said a patrolman in his statement, "were hit by other hippies who were throwing rocks at the police." Films reveal that when police were chasing demonstrators into Grant Park, one young man upended a sawhorse and heaved it at advancing officers. At one point the deputy superintendent of police was knocked down by a thrown sawhorse. At least one police three-wheeler was tipped over. One of the demonstrators says that "people in the park were prying up cobblestones and breaking them. One person piled up cobblestones in his arms and headed toward the police." Witnesses reported that people were throwing "anything they could lay their hands on. From the windows of the Hilton and Blackstone hotels, toilet paper, wet towels, even ash trays came raining down." A police lieutenant stated that he saw policemen bombarded with "rocks, cherry bombs, jars of vasoline, jars of mayonnaise and pieces of wood torn from the yellow barricades falling in the street." He, too, noticed debris falling from the hotel windows.

A number of police officers were injured, either by flying

missiles or in personal attacks. One, for example, was helping a fellow officer "pick up a hippie when another hippie
gave [me] a heavy kick, aiming for my groin." The blow
struck the officer partly on the leg and partly in the testi-
cles. He went down, and the "hippie" who kicked him
escaped.

In another instance, a Chicago police reporter said in his
statement, "a police officer reached down and grabbed a
person who dove forward and bit the officer on the leg. . . .
Three or four fellow policemen came to his aid. They had
to club the demonstrator to make him break his clamp on
the officer's leg." In another case, the witness saw a
demonstrator "with a big mop of hair hit a police officer
with an old British Army type metal helmet." The reporter
said he also heard "hissing sounds from the demonstrators
as if they were spraying the police." Later he found empty
lacquer spray and hair spray cans on the street. Also he
heard policemen cry out, "They're kicking us with knives
in their shoes." Later, he said, he found that demonstrators
"had actually inserted razor blades in their shoes."

By 8:15 p.m., the intersection was in police control. One
group of police proceeded east on Balbo, clearing the
street and splitting the crowd into two. Because National
Guard lines still barred passage over the Balbo Street
bridge, most of the demonstrators fled into Grant Park. A
Guardsman estimates that 5,000 remained in the park
across from the Hilton. Some clubbing by police occurred;
a demonstrator says he saw a brick hurled at police; but
few arrests were made.

Now, with police lines beginning to re-form, the deputy
superintendent directed the police units to advance north
on Michigan. He says announcements were again made to
clear the area and warnings given that those refusing to do
so would be arrested. To this, according to a patrolman
who was present, "The hippie group yelled 'fuck you' in
unison."

Police units formed up. National Guard intelligence

officers on the site called for Guard assistance. At 8:30 the Secret Service reported trucks full of Guard troops from Soldier Field moving north on Michigan Avenue to the Conrad Hilton and additional units arrived about 20 minutes later. The troops included the same units that had seen action earlier in the day after the bandshell rally and had later been moved to 22nd Street.

By 8:55 p.m., the Guard had taken up positions in a U-shaped formation, blocking Balbo at Michigan and paralleling the Hilton and Grant Park—a position that was kept until 4 a.m. Thursday. Although bayonets were affixed when the troops first hit the street, they were quickly removed. Explains a Guardsman who was there: "The bayonets had gotten in our way when we were on the Congress Street bridge." At one point, a demonstrator tried to "take the muzzle off" one of the Guardsmen's rifle. "All the time the demonstrators were trying to talk to us. They said 'join us' or 'fuck the draft.' We were told not to talk to anyone in the crowd." One Guard unit followed behind the police as a backup group.

With the police and Guard at its rear, the crowd fractured in several directions as it moved away from Balbo and Michigan. Near Michigan and Monroe another casualty center had been set up in the headquarters of the Church Federation of Greater Chicago. This, plus the melding of the crowds northbound on Michigan and east-bound on Monroe, brought about 1,000 persons to the west side of Michigan between Adams and Monroe, facing the Art Institute. There were few demonstrators on the east side of Michigan.

At 9:25 p.m., the police commander ordered a sweep of Michigan Avenue south from Monroe. At about this same time the police still had lines on both the west and east sides of Michigan in front of the Hilton and additional National Guard troops had arrived at 8th Street.

At 9:57 p.m., the demonstrators still on Michigan Avenue, prodded along by the southward sweep of the police, began marching back to Grant Park, chanting "Back to the park." By 10:10 p.m., an estimated 800 to 1,000 demonstrators had gathered in front of the Hilton.

By then, two city street sweeping trucks had rumbled up and down the street in front of the hotel, cleaning up the residue of violence—shoes, bottles, rocks, tear gas handkerchiefs. A police captain said the debris included: "Bases and pieces of broken bottles, a piece of board (1″ × 4″ × 14″), an 18-inch length of metal pipe, a 24-inch stick with a protruding sharpened nail, a 12-inch length of ½-inch diameter pipe, pieces of building bricks, an 18-inch stick with a razor blade protruding . . . several plastic balls somewhat smaller than tennis balls containing approximately 15 to 20 sharpened nails driven into the ball from various angles." When the delegates returned to the Hilton, they saw none of the litter of the battle.

As the crowd had dispersed from the Hilton the big war of Michigan and Balbo was, of course, over. But for those in the streets, as the rivulets of the crowd forked through the areas north of the hotel, there were still battles to be fought. Police violence and police baiting were some time in abating. Indeed, some of the most vicious incidents occurred in this "post-war" period.

The U.S. Attorney states that as the crowd moved north on Michigan Avenue, "they pelted the police with missiles of all sorts, rocks, bottles, firecrackers. When a policeman was struck, the crowd would cheer. The policemen in the line were dodging and jumping to avoid being hit." A police sergeant told the FBI that even a telephone was hurled from the crowd at the police.

In the first block north of the Hilton, recalls a man who was standing outside a Michigan Avenue restaurant, demonstrators "menaced limousines, calling the occupants 'scum,' telling them they didn't belong in Chicago and to go home."

As the police skirmish line moved north, and drew nearer to the squad cars, the lieutenant said, he saw several persons shoving paper through the cars' broken windows—in his opinion, a prelude to setting the cars on fire. A theology student who was in the crowd states that "a demonstrator took a fire extinguisher and sprayed inside the car. Then he put paper on the ground under the gas tank. . . . People shouted at him to stop." To break up the crowd, the lieutenant said, he squirted tear gas from an aerosol container and forced the demonstrators back.

"Two or three policemen, one with a white shirt, advanced on the crowd," one witness said, "The white-shirted one squirted mace in arcs back and forth before him."

A cameraman for the *Chicago Daily News* photographed a woman cowering after she had been sprayed with mace. A *News* representative states that the officer administering the mace, whom the photographers identified as a police lieutenant, then turned and directed the spray at the cameraman. The cameraman shot a photograph of this. The police lieutenant states that he does not remember this incident.

A priest who was in the crowd says he saw a "boy, about 14 or 15 white, standing on top of an automobile yelling something which was unidentifiable. Suddenly a policeman forced him down from the car and beat him to the ground by striking him three or four times with a nightstick. Other police joined in . . . and they eventually shoved him to a police van."

A well-dressed woman saw this incident and spoke angrily to a nearby police captain. As she spoke, another policeman came up from behind her and sprayed something in her face with an aerosol can. He then clubbed her to the ground. He and two other policemen then dragged her along the ground to the same paddy wagon and threw her in.

"At the corner of Congress Plaza and Michigan," states a doctor, "was gathered a group of people, number between 30 and 40. They were trapped against a railing by several policemen on motorcycles. The police charged the people on motorcycles and struck about a dozen of them, knocking several of them down. About 20 standing there jumped over the railing. On the other side of the railing was a three-to-four-foot drop. None of the people who were struck by the motorcycles appeared to be seriously injured. However, several of them were limping as if they had been run over on their feet."

A UPI reporter witnessed these attacks, too. He relates in his statement that one officer, "with a smile on his face and a fanatical look in his eyes, was standing on the three-wheel cycle, shouting, 'Wahoo, wahoo,' and trying to run down people on the sidewalk." The reporter says he was chased 30 feet by the cycle.

A few seconds later he "turned around and saw a policeman with a raised billy stick." As he swung around, the police stick grazed his head and struck his shoulders. As he was on his knees, he says someone stepped on his back.

A Negro policeman helped him to his feet, the reporter says. The policeman told him, "You know, man I didn't do this. One of the white cops did it." Then, the reporter quotes the officer as saying, "You know what? After this is all over, I'm quitting the force."

An instant later, the shouting officer on the motorcycle swung by again, and the reporter dove into a doorway for safety.

Near this same intersection, a Democratic delegate from Oklahoma was surrounded in front of his hotel by about ten persons, two of them with long hair and beards. He states that they encircled him for several minutes and subjected him to verbal abuse because they felt he "represented the establishment" and was "somewhat responsible for the alleged police brutality." The delegate stood mute and was eventually rescued by a policeman.

At Van Buren, a college girl states, "demonstrators were throwing things at passing police cars, and I saw one policeman hit in the face with a rock. A small paddy wagon drove up with only one policeman in it, and the crowd began rocking the wagon. The cop fell out and was surrounded by the crowd, but no effort was made to hurt him."

At Jackson, says the graduate student quoted earlier, "People got into the street on their knees and prayed, including several ministers who were dressed in clerical garb. These people, eight or ten of them, were arrested. This started a new wave of dissent among the demonstrators, who got angry. Many went forward to be arrested voluntarily; others were taken forcibly and some were beaten. . . . Objects were being thrown directly at police, including cans, bottles and paper."

"I was in the street," a witness who was near the intersection states, "when a fire in a trash basket appeared. . . . In a few minutes, two fire engines passed south through the crowd, turned west on Van Buren and stopped. They were followed by two police wagons which stopped in the middle of the block. As I walked north past the smaller of the two wagons, it began to rock." (The wagon also was being pelted by missiles, the U.S. Attorney states, and "PIGS" was painted on its sides.)

"I retreated onto the east sidewalk," the witness continued. Two policemen jumped out of the smaller wagon and one was knocked down by a few demonstrators, while other demonstrators tried to get these demonstrators away. The two policemen got back to the wagon, the crowd having drawn well back around them." The U.S. Attorney's report states that one of the policemen was "stomped" by a small group of the mob.

A young woman who was there and who had attended the bandshell rally earlier in the afternoon states that the crowd rocked the wagon for some time, while its officers stayed inside. "Then," she says, "the driver came out wildly swinging his club and shouting. About ten people jumped on him. He was kicked pretty severely and was downed. When he got up he was missing his club and his hat."

A police commander says that at about this moment he received "an urgent radio message" from an officer inside the van. He radioed that "demonstrators were standing on the hood of his wagon . . . and were preparing to smash the windshield with a baseball bat," the commander recalled. The officer also told him that the demonstrators were attempting to overturn the squadrol and that the driver "was hanging on the door in a state of shock." The commander told the officer that assistance was on the way.

"I heard a '10-1' call on either my radio or one of the other hand sets being carried by other men with me," the U.S. Attorney states, "and then heard, 'Car 100-sweep!' [Car 100 was assigned to the police commander.] With a roar of motors, squads, vans and three-wheelers came from east, west and north into the block north of Jackson."

"Almost immediately a CTA bus filled with police came over the Jackson Drive bridge and the police formed a line in the middle of the street," says a witness. "I heard shouts that the police had rifles and that they had cocked and pumped them. Demonstrators began to run."

"I ran north of Jackson . . . just as police were clearing the intersection and forming a line across Michigan," says the witness quoted above. "The police who had formed a line facing east in the middle of Michigan charged, yelling and clubbing into the crowd, running at individuals and groups who did not run before them."

"As the fray intensified around the intersection of Michigan and Jackson, a big group ran west on Jackson, with a group of blue-shirted policemen in pursuit, beating at them with clubs," says the U.S. Attorney's report. Some of the crowd ran up the alleys; some north on Wabash; and some west on Jackson to State with the police in pursuit."

An Assistant U.S. Attorney later reported that "the

demonstrators were running as fast as they could but were unable to get out of the way because of the crowds in front of them. I observed the police striking numerous individuals, perhaps 20 or 30. I saw three fall down and then be overrun by the police. I observed two demonstrators who had multiple cuts on their heads. We assisted one who was in shock into a passer-by's car.

"A TV mobile truck appeared . . . and the police became noticeably more restrained, holding their clubs at waist level rather than in the air," a witness relates. "As the truck disappeared . . . the head-clubbing tactics were resumed."

One demonstrator states that he ran off Michigan Avenue on to Jackson. He says he and his wife ran down Jackson and were admitted, hesitantly, into a restaurant. They seated themselves at a table by the window facing onto Jackson and, while sitting at the table, observed a group of people running down Jackson with policemen following them and striking generally at the crowd with their batons. At one instance, he saw a policeman strike a priest in the head with a baton.

At the intersection of Jackson and Wabash, said a student whose wife was beaten in the race from Michigan, "the police came from all four directions and attacked the crowd. Demonstrators were beaten and run to the paddy wagons. I saw a black policeman go berserk. He charged blindly at the group of demonstrators and made two circles through the crowd, swinging wildly at anything."

An Assistant U.S. Attorney watching the action on various side streets reported, "I observed police officers clearing people westward . . . using their clubs to strike people on the back of the head and body on several occasions. Once a policeman ran alongside a young girl. He held her by the shoulder of her jacket and struck at her a few times as they were both running down the sidewalk.

A traffic policeman on duty on Michigan Avenue says

that the demonstrators who had continued north often surrounded cars and buses attempting to move south along Michigan Avenue. Many males in the crowd, he says, exposed their penises to passers-by and other members of the crowd. They would run up to cars clogged by the crowd and show their private parts to the passengers.

To men, the officer says, they shouted such questions as, "How would you like me to fuck your wife?" and "How would you like to fuck a man?" Many of the demonstrators also rocked the automobiles in an effort to tip them over. A policeman states that bags of feces and urine were dropped on the police from the building.

As the crowd moved south again on Michigan, a traffic policeman, who was in the vicinity of Adams Street, recalls, "They first took control of the lions in front of the Art Institute. They climbed them and shouted things like, "Let's fuck" and "Fuck, fuck, fuck!" At this same intersection, an officer rescued two Loop secretaries from being molested by demonstrators. He asked them, "What are you doing here?" They replied, "We wanted to see what the hippies were like." His response: "How do you like what you saw?"

While all that was going on in and around Grant Park, Lincoln Park on Wednesday was quiet and uncrowded; but there was sporadic violence in Old Town again that night. Two University of Minnesota students who wandered through the park in the morning say they heard small groups of demonstrators saying things like "Fuck the pigs," and "Kill them all," but by this time that was not unusual. They also heard a black man addressing a group of demonstrators. He outlined plans for the afternoon, and discussed techniques for forming skirmish lines, disarming police officers, and self defense.

Also during the morning Abbie Hoffman was arrested at the Lincoln Hotel Coffee Shop, 1800 North Clark, and charged with resisting arrest and disorderly conduct. According to Hoffman's wife, Anita, she and her husband

and a friend were eating breakfast when three policemen entered the coffee shop and told Hoffman they had received three complaints about an obscene word written on Hoffman's forehead. The word was "Fuck." Hoffman says he printed the word on his forehead to keep cameramen from taking his picture.

Most of the violence against police, from all reports, was the work of gang-type youths called "greasers." They dismantled police barricades to lure squad cars down Stockton Drive, where one observer says "punks engaged in some of the most savage attacks on police that had been seen." Ministers and hippies in the area were directing traffic around the barricades and keeping people from wandering into the danger area. Two ministers in particular were trying to "keep the cool."

By 10:30 p.m., most of the action was centered once more in Grant Park across from the Hilton, where several hundred demonstrators and an estimated 1,500 spectators gathered to listen to what one observer describes as "unexciting speeches." There was the usual singing and shouting. Twice during the evening police and Hilton security officers went into the hotel and went to quarters occupied by McCarthy personnel—once to protest the ripping of sheets to bandage persons who had been injured and a second time to try to locate persons said to be lobbing ashtrays out of the windows. But compared to the earlier hours of the evening, the rest of the night was quiet.

In Grant Park, the sullen crowd sat facing the hotel. Someone with a transistor radio was listening to the roll call vote of states on the nomination and broadcasting the count to the rest of the throng over a bullhorn. There were loud cheers for Ted Kennedy, McCarthy, McGovern and Phillips ("He's a black man," said the youth with the bullhorn.) Boos and cries of "Dump the Hump" arose whenever Humphrey received votes. "When Illinois was called," says the trained observer, "no one could hear totals because of booing and the chant, 'To Hell with Daley.' "

During this time the police line was subject to considerable verbal abuse from within the crowd and a witness says that both black and white agitators at the edge of the crowd tried to kick policemen with razor blades embedded in their shoes. Periodically several policemen would make forays into the crowd, punishing demonstrators they thought were involved.

At about "Louisiana," as the roll call vote moved with quickening pace toward the climax of Humphrey's nomination, the crowd grew restless, recalls a trained observer. About this same time, according to the Log, the police skirmish line began pushing the demonstrators farther east into the park. A report of an officer being struck by a nail ball was received by police. Film taken at about this time shows an officer being hit by a thrown missile, later identified as a chunk of concrete with a steel reinforcement rod in it. The blow knocked him down and, as he fell, the crowd cheered and yelled, "More!" The chant, "Kill the pigs," filled the air.

"At 'Oklahoma,' " recalls an observer, "the Yippie on the bullhorn said, 'Marshals ready. Don't move. Stay seated.' "

"The front line rose [facing the police] and locked arms, and the others stayed seated. Humphrey was over the top with Pennsylvania, and someone in the Hilton rang a cow bell at the demonstrators. Boos went up, as did tension. A bus load of police arrived. Others standing in front of the Hilton crossed Michigan and lined up behind those in front of the demonstrators.

"The chant of 'Sit down, sit down' went out. An American flag was raised on a pole upside down. Wandering began among demonstrators and the chant continued.

Shortly before midnight, while Benjamin Ortiz was speaking, National Guard troops of the 2/129 Inf. came west on Balbo to Michigan to replace the police in front of the Hilton. "For the first time," says an observer, "machine guns mounted on trucks were pulled up directly in front of the demonstrators, just behind the police lines. The machine guns, and the Guard's mesh-covered jeeps with barbed wire fronts made the demonstrators angry and nervous. Bayonets were readied. In films of this period the word "pig" can be seen written on the street.

"Ortiz continued, 'Dig this man, just 'cause you see some different pigs coming here, don't get excited. We're going to sleep here, sing here, sex here, live here!' "

As the police moved off, one of the first Guard maneuvers was to clear demonstrators from Michigan's east sidewalk. This was done to allow pedestrian traffic. The crowd reacted somewhat hostilely to the maneuver, but by and large, the demonstrators semed to view the Guard as helpless men who had been caught up in the events and did not treat them as badly as they had the police. Having secured the sidewalk, the guards shortly retired to the east curb of Michigan Avenue. A line of "marshals" sat down at the edge of the grass at the feet of the guards. Access to the hotel was restored and people began to move from the hotel to the park and vice versa. By now, there were an estimated 4,000 persons assembled across from the Hilton. Most of the crowd sat down in a mass and became more orderly, singing "America" and "God Bless America." McCarthy supporters joined the crowd and were welcomed.

By 12:20 a.m., Thursday, the crowd had declined to 1,500 and was considered under control. By 12:33 a.m., the police department had retired from the streets and the Guard took over the responsibility of holding Michingan from Balbo to 8th Street. At 12:47 a.m., another contingent of Guard troops arrived at the Hilton. Delegates were returning and were being booed unless they could be identified as McCarthy or McGovern supporters. Those delegates were cheered and asked to join the group.

The crowd grew in number. By 1:07 a.m., the Secret Service estimated 2,000 persons in the park across from the hotel. Ten minutes later the crowd had grown by another

500. Those in the park were "listening to speeches—orderly" according to the log.

January 1969

Breakdown in Law and Order

TOM PARMENTER

Spokesmen and public men, preachers and newspaper columnists need only open their mouths in the face of a Detroit or a Newark or a Watts and the phrase "breakdown of law and order" comes rolling out. The cliche has much to commend it to such men. Certainly neither "They're breeding like hamsters down there" or "We need to set up a pilot program" quite covers the situation and until the time comes to say "We must appoint a committee" nothing is quite so appropriate as "breakdown."

Cliches are convenient. No one in love or in mourning uses anything else. And as shorthand expressions of public figures they make the work of a reporter lighter. The danger comes when the cliche becomes reality, when it turns into an explanation. In the case of Detroit and the other urban riots, "breakdown of law and order" means looting and snipers, soup lines, broken windows and broken lives, corpses and sirens, and calling out the troops. This is the meaning of the phrase to the public men who use it, but the phrase may have another meaning to the Negroes of Detroit.

I spent several days in Detroit as the riots were running down gathering material on encounters with the police. What appears below is not the truth that may eventually emerge from trials, grand-jury investigations, and committees, but the truth as perceived by those involved in the events.

The Detroit riots started in a police raid on what is known locally with self-conscious quaintness as a blind pig, an after-hours tavern. The police began to move the eighty patrons to the precinct station for booking and downtown to jail. The police guard around the building attracted a crowd even at 5 a.m. Someone smashed the window of a squad car. Within minutes the crowd began to move down 12th Street breaking windows and looting. A shoe store was torched and the crowd grew. One of the first official acts of the police commissioner was to block off Belle Isle Park, the island which saw the worst of the 1943 riot. Despite the trouble, the night police watch went off duty as usual at 8 a.m. and the day watch came on. At the same time, things began to quiet down a bit. The crowd milled around the streets, good-tempered if sarcastic. The police increased their guard.

"They were intimidating the hell out of the streets, man," said a Negro community organizer who was on 12th Street that Sunday morning. "It was the most insane thing you'd want to see. They just occupied 12th Street. Ninety God-damn degrees, Sunday morning, and they just occupy that street. They thought about pulling off but they waited until too late. The tension was bad, man. And the police recognized it and said, 'Well, maybe we'd better get out of here a little bit,' you know? Between 9 a.m. and the time they pulled some of the police out, that's when it really got going. Cats was walking up and down the streets drinking blood and saying 'We're going to burn it. We're going to smoke it up and we don't want nobody down there talking no shit.' "

"It was just too late. It would have erupted sooner or later. There was nothing to do *then*. I mean it was all over. What they should have done when they busted that blind pig and these cats broke in those three stores, they should have boarded those stores up and got the hell out of there and then sent some detectives in there or something. But these cats boarded the damned things up and blocked off 12th Street and when people came out in the morning here they are with shotguns on the God-damned streets. If that's not the most stupid thing. They just made mistake after mistake. And they miscalculated in so God-damn many areas. I mean it can only go so long. I mean the probability of this kind of thing happening under the *law enforcement* process here in Detroit. It was time for something to happen. These cats have gotten away with so much shit, man. They ran down Negroes on *horses* in Belle Isle last year, man. There was no riot until these cats started it. They tried to start the riot four days earlier down on Butternut."

The incident referred to took place about three miles from the blind pig. A disturbance had started over a disorderly conduct arrest. "They called in the rest of the dogs down there, man. In four minutes, it was 20 squad cars in that block. Police was all over the place, you know. And there they was with these shotguns, all prepared with riot tactics. It was an integrated crowd standing around watching, you know. It was irresponsibility. Four days later they did the same damned thing on 12th Street but they was in the wrong part of town. It blew up.

"The *whole thing* was showing force. That's all they was doing was showing force, intimidating purposely. The policy of showing force went straight on to the other end, man. Three hours after these cats were showing force with the Detroit police department down here on 12th Street, the law had broke down completely."

The riot started again in full force about noon on Sunday. A young man described for me his usual way of life and his part in the riots. Call him Arthur.

"I'm making more money than the average white man with a white collar job," he said.

"How is that?"

"Well, I make mine."

"Hustling?"

"Well," he smiled and went on, "I do a little bit of everything. I don't steal for it. I don't rob nobody. I mean I can't go to jail unless somebody tell on me, you understand? And I don't think they're going to tell on me because they love me."

"How did you hear about the riot?"

"I heard a friend of mine say, 'Hey! They rioting up on 12th.' I said what are they doing and he said *looting*. That's all it *took* to get me *out* of the house. He said the police was letting them take it; they wasn't stopping it; so I said it was time for me to get some of these diamonds and watches and rings. It wasn't that I was mad at anybody or angry or trying to get back at the white man. If I saw something that I could get without getting hurt, I got it."

Arthur's assertion that he wasn't trying to get back at anyone was not assured. He did agree that he was stealing.

"This is nothing but pure lawlessness. People are trying to get what they can get. They *have* been *denied* these things and when the first brick was thrown, that's all it took. Let's get it while we can get it. They were trying to get all they could get. They got diamonds here, they got money here, they got clothes here and TV's and what not. What could they do with it when they bring it out except sell it to each other? That's all. They're just getting something they haven't got. I mean, I bought me some clothes from somebody. I have exchanged whiskey and different things for different things. You know, something I wanted that I didn't have. This was a good way to get it. *I really enjoyed myself.*

"I didn't get caught until Sunday night. I got caught because I was going into one of them little bitty stores instead of going in one of them big stores. I went to a stocking store because I was going to get my girl friend some stockings. I had three or four hundred pair under my arm when I come out. They told me to put 'em down.

"Before that the police weren't stopping me. What have we got them for? They *could* have stopped it. I'd come up and I'd have an armful of clothes or a bagful of diamonds and he'd say, 'Having fun?' I'd say 'Plenty of it.' I'd take them on and go back and get some more. If he had pulled a gun and said drop it it would have been dropped. I wouldn't have picked up nothing else. But they seemed to be enjoying seeing 12th Street tore down."

"Why?"

"For the prostitutes. That's the *only* reason. It's more prostitutes than it is people living there.

"I thought it was a lot of fun. People see'n what they could get for nothing and they went out and got it. It wasn't no race riot. They was white and Negro both going in stores and helping each other pass things out. Having a good time. Really enjoying themselves until them *fools* [snipers] started shooting. I hope they can get them because they're stopping me from making my money.

"Before that you didn't even have to go in a store to get nothing. All you had to do was tell people you saw with a bunch of stuff, 'Hey buddy, let me get some of that.' They'd give you some. One guy had ten suits and I had two; he gave me three. That's the way it was. It wasn't no organized stuff. Everybody was trying to get in it. I went in one place there was about 10 hands in a safe trying to get the money. Like I said, I really enjoyed myself.

"The only thing was that we had a minority group that was going around burning. I really do believe it was organized. They waited until stuff got going. See? What they tried to do was shoot off a few police officers and see if everybody would get armed. That's ridiculous."

The snipers in Detroit 1967—there were snipers there in 1943 as well—attracted a great deal of attention, and not only from adherents of devil theories. It is widely believed by Detroit officials that fewer than a dozen snipers —white and Negro—ever fired a gun in Detroit during the riots. Although police reports make frequent mention of sniper fire in the area of a number of the riot deaths, even the daily tally issued during the riots by police attributed only two deaths to sniper fire. In comparison, 22 deaths were attributed to shootings by police, soldiers, private guards, and store owners. Of these, 14 were killed by the Detroit police. All the deaths occurred after the first day of looting described above.

Three of the deaths for which the police nominated snipers as a probable source may become a greater cause celebre than the riots themselves. Three days after I gathered most of the following material, the deaths hit the front pages of the Detroit papers. The implication was police execution. Since then, several investigations of the incident have been announced.

The first police reports implied that three youths had been killed in an exchange of gunfire between police and snipers in an annex to the Algiers Motel. (The annex is located on a pleasant tree-lined street not at all untypical of Detroit's Negro neighborhoods.) No guns were found in the rooms where the bodies were found, however, and the police were informed of the deaths anonymously—not by an official source.

One witness was Michael Clark, 19. His roommate, Carl Cooper, 17, was killed. "There was no shooting around the motel at all. We was just sitting in the room doing nothing. The first shooting I knew about came from the cops. I looked out and there was a state trooper pointing a rifle up into the window. Carl ran down the hall. I guess they shot him downstairs. That's where the body was. He was dead when we got down. They said they was going to shoot us one at a time. Called us niggers. I heard them shoot Fred Temple after they took him out. They just kept on beating us and beating us all the time. Then they told me to come into a room and they pointed a gun in my face. Told me to lay down and then he shot. He shot above me. I don't know why he didn't shoot me. Then I heard another shot across the hall. I guess that was Aubrey Pollard when they shot him. I don't know why they did it. I got out of there. But I'm going to testify. I've already talked to the detectives."

Cooper's funeral was a Jessica Mitford affair held in a funeral home so "tasteful" that it looked like an architect's drawing rather than a building in use. Clark was one of the pallbearers. "I knew Carl since we was little kids."

Cooper's family and friends seemed the sort known as "the good people of the Negro community." They were decorous people, well-dressed and driving good cars. They were not necessarily middle class, but they were urban people, not poverty-stricken Southern migrants dressed uncomfortably in their mail-order suits and Sunday dresses. The body was lying in an open coffin. The minister offered his comforting best to a background of weeping. After everyone had passed the body, curtains were drawn across the front of the room, hiding the pulpit and the body. Suddenly, the room erupted in a surge of emotion. Women screamed and several charged the curtain only to be led away by attendants. The family seating section lost all semblance of regularity as women began to rock back and forth and soon everyone was moving around the room. The funeral director eyed his watch; another cortege was waiting to move into the chapel. The women who had been led away went back into the room. The minister offered more words and then the curtains were reopened and Clark and the other pallbearers moved the coffin out to the hearse.

The stories about investigations of the death were not yet public, but they were common knowledge among the several hundred gathered for Cooper's funeral. In fact, the stories were being heard all over the West side soon after the deaths early Wednesday. Arthur, the hustler quoted above, hangs around the Algiers and although he was unwilling to admit it to himself, it was only happenstance that he was not killed himself.

Arthur wasn't at Cooper's funeral, although he said he was closer to him than to the other two who were killed. His ambivalence about race is apparent as he talks about politics and grief. "I think Johnson is for the Negroes. He has to be to be President. I would be for anybody in the world if they was going to elect me President. Everybody's talking about Abe Lincoln freeing the slaves but there was only one man who was really for the Negroes and that was Kennedy. You see what they did to him. That's the only man—white man, black man, green man—that I ever cried for when he got killed. That was the man."

"Did you cry over these kids?"

"Naw. I didn't cry over them. I mean, that's life. They wasn't doing anything for me. Kennedy was trying to help me. I felt bad about them, but the first thing that hit my mind was, 'I'm glad it wasn't me.' That's the only thing I thought about."

His first words when asked about the shootings were, "It was murder. They just murdered them boys. They just happened to be with these white girls, all of them sitting up in the room together. That's what it was. We was standing outside and the guard here at the motel said it's curfew time and we had to get in. So they went around with them and we went on in our place. That's the deal.

"There were plenty of cops around. When we opened the door to see—we heard some shooting—just a crack more or less and a shotgun or a rifle came into the door and told us to come on out of there. That's what we did. I didn't know who it was and I didn't care. I was coming out even if it had been a sniper, but I was coming out.

"When the other bunch come downstairs one of them was in the hall already dead. That's Carl. I know for a fact that Carl was not the kind of guy to be raising no whole lot of hell. If a policeman put a drop on him he's going to raise them up like he's supposed to. He was dead. They killed him. Then they shot the other two and then just called downtown and said it's three bodies up in back of the Algiers. They didn't do no reporting other than that, no numbers or saying they was policemen or nothing.

"There wasn't any rioting or anything closer than six

blocks away. I did hear about some blank pistol or something being shot but that wasn't close." [Newspaper reports stated that Cooper had a starter's pistol, but none was found.]

Arthur continued: "I think it must be because the white girls was in the room with them. I really do. It was just cold-blooded murder. They asked the girls, 'Which one of you white whores is fucking one of these black niggers?' Before the girl could say something he hit her in the head. He beat her down. They hit her in the head with the rifle."

A second young man—he gave his name as Boston Blackie and said he was a pimp—broke into the conversation. "I'm going to tell you what the whole deal was. They probably didn't know how it happened, seeing these white girls in this room with these Negroes. They didn't give nobody a chance to explain themselves. All cops are probably prejudiced to an extent. This girl that was hit told me the officer was in the late thirties or early forties. She said he seemed like he was nuts. She said he came in talking that shit about a white woman in there. At first I didn't believe it when I heard it. Then I was sick when I came over and found out. They said this one guy who was giving the orders seemed like he was mentally unbalanced or something. The dude *had* to be crazy. He was talking about who wants to die first the girls or the fellows. She thought he was going to shoot her, too, after he hit her on the head."

Arthur continued: "They had us all out there in the court by the swimming pool. They didn't tell us to lay down or nothing. I asked *them* if there was going to *be* any shooting to let me lay down. I didn't want to be standing up because they had jeeps out here with these 50 calibers pointed this way and I didn't want them to shoot me. I was already scared of being shot at. It was a half hour after they laid us down that we found out that the boys was dead. One of the security guards around the motel walked one of the girls back to her room and when they walked in the hallway the boys was in there dead. The police had gone.

"They left the bodies here. You wouldn't expect them to stay after committing murder. The boys was laying down when they shot them. They looked for bullet holes and couldn't find them till they looked on the floor.

"I really thought Michael was dead. That's what they told me. I really thought he was dead until he showed up today. He came in here and said, 'Well, I'm not dead, y'all.'

"Now why did all this happen? What kind of shit is this? They don't turn in no report on who they are or nothing. That's nothing but murder. That's all it was and all it could be.

"If the boys *was* up there shooting *out* the window, *get on up there* and shoot *in* the window. Don't be just shooting all over the place. They could kill anybody. They had the boys in there and they had them up against the wall. They could have called the paddy wagon or whatever they wanted and took them downtown. They didn't have to kill the boys. They had no business over there. They wasn't doing shit in that room. They wasn't even playing cards like we was. They said they heard some shots and that's all it took. If I had had a cap pistol they'd be liable to come in there shooting instead of saying 'what is it' or 'come on out.' They just went in shooting."

"They just went in shooting." The words were repeated to describe one of the last deaths in the riot. The following material was gathered less than an hour after the death, at the same time that the street was hearing it first.

An inquest or trial may turn up a different and perhaps more correct story, but a story that will be heard by dozens as compared to the far greater number who heard the story as it appears here.

Of all those killed in the riots in Detroit, regular army paratroopers killed one, this one. The national guardsmen killed three, according to a police summary. Policemen are accustomed to working alone or with a partner. The closest they get to tactics—and it happens rarely in the normal course of police work—is surrounding a house with a single man holed up inside. Soldiers, on the other hand, rarely work in units smaller than a squad. The paratrooper who killed Ernest Roquemore this night—by accident it would seem—was one of the few army men who had been removed from his unit and assigned to a police car. The policeman he was working with wounded a youth and two girls, 13 and 17, with his personal hunting weapon, a 16-gauge shotgun.

Police said they were looking for loot. One of the injured girls had been visiting the apartment of her brother where the shootings took place. Their father is talking.

"My wife was talking to my daughter on the phone when it happened. My wife just heard a shot on the phone. She said, 'John, please, something done happened already. Please go over to Hal's house (which is my son). Somebody's done shot somebody.' I got here as fast as I could and they wouldn't let me in. They said it was looting. There was some looting around the corner, but my son, he don't believe in looting. Like they said that furniture was looted. But that furniture wasn't looted. I've got to pay. I've got the receipt. My son put $800 down on that furniture and he still owes $592. They wouldn't let him get it because he owes for an automobile. So I had to co-sign for him. I got the book here. We paid regular. They said he had to put that heavy payment down for the furniture.

"They said there was somebody in there with a gun. Maybe there was, but I didn't see him. Then they said they was some marijuana. I don't know."

Roquemore, 19, a resident of the building, was shot accidentally while the paratrooper was firing at an armed youth who was running away. He was not caught, but police said they found a packet of marijuana on the stairs.

The father continued: "They just bust in there without saying nothing to nobody. Now I come over here and they won't tell me anything. They said, 'Well, you can't go in there.' I said, 'Why not? I want to see who's hurt because my son stays here. I want to see what's the matter.' They said, 'Naw, you have to stay on the side.' Then this Negro soldier, he said, 'Look, do like they say. Don't get yourself involved. Take it easy. So many of my people getting killed already.' I stood back there. I obeyed them. Then I waited and they tried to take the furniture out. I got the book right here. I'm waiting for them now. They can't take that furniture out because it belongs to my son.

"I don't know about that marijuana or that looting or what. I don't see where that give them the right to be shooting when they come in the house. They should find out who's *in there* first.

"There's four people shot. They said somebody had a gun. But didn't nobody up there shoot at nobody. Maybe they thought somebody was breaking in and then if I had a gun I might get it out. But the policemen didn't say nothing. They just came in shooting.

"This is worser than the thing, the raid, that started the riots. Didn't nobody do nothing but they just go in there shooting. Then they want to say, 'How come the colored man get down wrong?' That make any man do something wrong."

The institution of the booster, the organizer, is a familiar one. One corporation front man I know introduces himself as "the vice president in charge of joining good causes." The adherents of this institution—which include the Babbitt, the PR man, the associate minister, and other assorted icon polishers—have generally been hired for their winning smiles and friction-free personalities.

More recently, the institution has been enlivened by a band of men who neither smile much nor avoid friction. Although Detroit may have been a little behind other cities, it is now home to a number of black community organizers. These men saw the riots as an opportunity to assert leadership in building a community. They were excited by the riots and proud of them in a way, but they were also depressed at the implication that rioting might present more opportunities than community organization.

Frank Ditto came to Detroit from Chicago just a month before the riots to work for a new group called CESSA, Churches on the East Side for Social Action. He was in Newark at the Black Power convention when the riots broke out in Detroit. He had gained fame in Chicago as the leader of 150 consecutive days of miles-long marches through the streets, ending each night at the home of Mayor Richard J. Daley. One of the first friends Ditto made in Detroit was Rennie Freeman, the executive director of the West Community Organization, an older counterpart to CESSA in the area that was most seriously hit by the riots. Whenever Ditto and Freeman meet they give one another the Black-Power secret grip, a variation on Indian wrestling.

Freeman was working on 12th Street when the riot began to emerge. John Conyers, the Negro Democrat who represents the West Side in Congress, asked Freeman to help quiet the crowds shortly before noon on Sunday. Freeman tells the story:

"Conyers and his functionaries came down here talking to me saying, 'Will you help?' I said, 'Man, I'll help you if you do the right thing.' He said, 'Well, I'm going to get a bullhorn down here and get these cats off the streets. We don't want anybody hurt.' So I said no. He said, 'What are you doing down here then? What are you here for? Do you want a riot?' You've got all these brothers down on the street corner and as I told Conyers, 'If you go up and down 12th Street with a bullhorn trying to tell all the colored folks to get off *their* street when these cops are standing out here with shotguns and bayonets, what's going to happen is that the people are going to turn against *you*.' I said I'd help if the police were going to get out, too, but I think even at that point it was too late. The young brothers was out there and they didn't dig it *at all*.

"I started walking down the street with the cat and here I am with John on one side and this functionary on the other. I said to myself, 'Well, hell, I'm not walking down here with these armband Negroes. What do I look like riding up and down 12th Street telling these cats to get off the street with these functionaries? John just can't comprehend that the disorganized brothers have something to say. He thinks that if you aren't organized you have nothing to say. So he made the mistake, but at that he was the only cat down there. None of these other Negro politicians was there. Conyers was the only one."

Regardless of the difficulty of organizing the "disorganized brothers," both Ditto and Freeman place their faith in organization. Said Ditto, "To be honest with myself, having been oppressed and subjected to all the dehumanizing factors of American life as a black man, I very well could have been out there burning, looting, and sniping. I see more point in organizing than I do in looting. It's more constructive. This kind of thing here, the rioting, runs out of gas in four or five days. With an organization when you get weak and tired you know that you have someone beside you who you can lean up against and still keep going on."

Ditto's mood varied widely. In an interview given a television reporter while the riots were still going on, organization, except in a special sense, was not foremost in his mind.

"Is this organized or a spontaneous thing?" the reporter asked.

"It's a combination of both. It was spontaneous in the sense that it was caused by just another incident of police brutality. It was organized in the sense that it has been going on more than four hundred years and the black folks have been organized for four hundred years to fight for survival."

He was even willing during the riots to take a realpolitik view of the loss of Negro lives and property in the riot.

"The way that society looks at these things, we would say it's unfortunate, but the United States is dropping napalm bombs on women and children over in Viet Nam and no one has anything to say about it. I mean, this is a state of war. This is the price of war. You might get killed and I might get killed and who gives a damn?"

A few days later, Ditto encountered two young hustlers who had enjoyed the rioting, but who were unwilling to extract any political moral from it.

"If they wanted to do something, really wanted to cut it up, why did they do it down here," one said. "In all these soup lines and burned apartments up and down 12th Street, all I see is colored people in a fix. They should have gone up to Grosse Pointe. Get in their cars and go up there and riot. That'd show somebody something. Not like this; this didn't show the white people nothing."

Organization was not for the hustlers. "The white man's got everything," one said. "I'd like to get in on it but I can't get in on it so I get around it. What's the old saying, 'God bless the child that's got his own'? The Negroes have just got to get out and get theirs like I'm getting mine. Let them go for theirself."

Ditto didn't like it. "Do you realize that just 150 years ago when black babies were born and brought into the earth the slave master would snatch them away from their mother and send them off to some other plantation as soon as they were old enough? They separated brothers and sisters and fathers and sons. Negroes don't stick together because of the psychological brainwashing they've been through for hundreds of years."

"I'll tell you one thing," the hustler replied. "It would have been hard to get me over here at all if my brother in Africa hadn't been selling me for some beads."

Despite this sort of apathy, Ditto and Freeman were planning to try to bring together young Negroes like these—and others even tougher and less articulate—with the hope of formulating a program of police-community relations. Freeman explained, "We've got to strike while the iron is hot. Right now nobody knows what the hell to do. But the brothers can tell them what to do without hesitating. The brothers know what needs to be done.

"They aren't going to hear it from these Uncle Tom preachers. They don't even know what the *gossip* is on

12th Street. This is the time to organize. Everybody's together if you leave out the Toms. The Negroes in the community belong to what's happening, man. Those rioters was running down the streets and I see these middle class people standing out on the porches giving the Black Power sign. You know, women in house dresses giving the fist. And it is clear that this thing about the lower class being disenchanted is bullshit. Negroes are disenchanted. It's not just the cats that have got the guts to throw the bricks that's pissed off. Everybody is pissed off. There these chicks are that sit on the PTA boards giving the Black Power sign when there's smoke all around. Even the Toms break down and cry. They just don't have no goddam guts. That's the only difference."

This was on one of their hopeful days. The next day, after attending the funeral of a Negro youth apparently killed by police during the rioting, Ditto's mood was one of despair. "I've had people treat me like that cigaret butt there just because I'm black. I could very easily be on the other side of the street with a 30-30 rifle. I have this fight with myself every day. I keep having this hope that people will somehow come to their senses. I don't know what I'll be doing a year from now. I might give up on this organizing. I just don't know what I'll do."

September 1967

Police Brutality...
Answers to Key Questions

ALBERT J. REISS, JR.

"For three years, there has been through the courts and the streets a dreary procession of citizens with broken heads and bruised bodies against few of whom was violence needed to effect an arrest. Many of them had done nothing to deserve an arrest. In a majority of such cases, no complaint was made. If the victim complains, his charge is generally dismissed. The police are practically above the law."

This statement was published in 1903, and its author was the Hon. Frank Moss, a former police commissioner of New York City. Clearly, today's charges of police brutality and mistreatment of citizens have a precedent in American history—but never before has the issue of police brutality assumed the public urgency it has today. In Newark, in Detroit, in Watts, in Harlem, and, in fact, in practically every city that has had a civil disturbance, "deep hostility between police

57

and ghetto" was, reports the Kerner Commission, "a primary cause of the riots."

Whether or not the police accept the words "police brutality," the public now wants some plain answers to some plain questions. How widespread is police mistreatment of citizens? Is it on the increase? Why do policemen mistreat citizens? Do the police mistreat Negroes more than whites?

To find some answers, 36 people working for the Center of Research on Social Organization observed police-citizen encounters in the cities of Boston, Chicago, and Washington, D.C. For seven days a week, for seven weeks during the summer of 1966, these observers, with police permission, sat in patrol cars and monitored booking and lockup ' procedures in high-crime precincts.

Obtaining information about police mistreatment of citizens is no simple matter. National and state civil-rights commissions receive hundreds of complaints charging mistreatment—but proving these allegations is difficult. The few local civilian-review boards, such as the one in Philadelphia, have not produced any significant volume of complaints leading to the dismissal or disciplining of policemen for alleged brutality. Generally, police chiefs are silent on the matter, or answer charges of brutality with vague statements that they will investigate any complaints brought to their attention. Rank-and-file policemen are usually more outspoken: They often insinuate that charges of brutality are part of a conspiracy against them, and against law and order.

What citizens mean by police brutality covers the full range of police practices. These practices, contrary to the impression of many civil-rights activists, are not newly devised to deal with Negroes in our urban ghettos. They are ways in which the police have traditionally behaved in dealing with certain citizens, particularly those in the lower classes. The most common of these practices are:

—the use of profane and abusive language,

—commands to move on or get home,

—stopping and questioning people on the street or searching them and their cars,

—threats to use force if not obeyed,

—prodding with a nightstick or approaching with a pistol, and

—the actual use of physical force or violence itself.

Citizens and the police do not always agree on what constitutes proper police practice. What is "proper," or what is "brutal," it need hardly be pointed out, is more a matter of judgment about what someone did than a description of what police do. What is important is not the practice itself but what it means to the citizen. What citizens object to and call "police brutality" is really the judgment that they have not been treated with the full rights and dignity owing citizens in a democratic society. Any practice that degrades their status, that restricts their freedom, that annoys or harasses them, or that uses physical force is frequently seen as unnecessary and unwarranted. More often than not, they are probably right.

Many police practices serve only to degrade the citizen's sense of himself and his status. This is particularly true with regard to the way the police use language. Most citizens who have contact with the police object less to their use of four-letter words than to *how* the policeman talks to them. Particularly objectionable is the habit policemen have of "talking down" to citizens, of calling them names that deprecate them in their own eyes and those of others. More than one Negro citizen has complained: "They talk down to me as if I had no name—like 'boy' or 'man' or whatever, or they call me 'Jack' or by my first name. They don't show me no respect."

Members of minority groups and those seen as nonconformists, for whatever reason, are the most likely targets of status degradation. Someone who has been drinking may be told he is a "bum" or a "shitty wino." A woman walking alone may be called a "whore." And a man who doesn't happen to meet a policeman's standard of how one should look or dress may be met with the remark, "What's the matter, you a queer?" A white migrant from the South may be called a "hillbilly" or "shitkicker"; a Puerto Rican, a "pork chop"; a young boy, a "punk kid." When the policeman does not use words of status degradation, his manner may be degrading. Citizens want to be treated as people, not as "nonpersons" who are talked about as if they were not present.

That many Negroes believe that the police have degraded their status is clear from surveys in Watts, Newark, and Detroit. One out of every five Negroes in our center's post-riot survey in Detroit reports that the police have "talked down to him." More than one in ten says a policeman has "called me a bad name."

To be treated as "suspicious" is not only degrading, but is also a form of harassment and a restriction on the right to move freely. The harassing tactics of the police—dispersing social street-gatherings, the indiscriminate stopping of Negroes on foot or in cars, and commands to move on or go home—are particularly common in ghetto areas.

Young people are the most likely targets of harassing orders to disperse or move on. Particularly in summer, ghetto youths are likely to spend lots of time in public places. Given the inadequacy of their housing and the absence of community facilities, the street corner is often their social center. As the police cruise the busy streets of the ghetto, they frequently shout at groups of teenagers to "get going" or "get home." Our observations of police practices show that *white as well as Negro youths* are often harassed in this way.

Frequently the policeman may leave the car and threaten or force youths to move on. For example, one summer evening as the scout car cruised a busy street of a white slum, the patrolmen observed three white boys and a girl on a corner. When told to move on, they mumbled and grumbled in undertones, angering the police by their failure to comply. As they slowly moved off, the officers pushed them along the street. Suddenly one of the white patrolmen took a lighted cigarette from a 15-year-old boy and stuck it in his face, pushing him forward as he did so. When the youngsters did move on, one policeman remarked to the observer that the girl was "nothing but a whore." Such tactics can only intensify resentment toward the police.

Police harassment is not confined to youth. One in every four adult Negroes in Detroit claims he has been stopped and questioned by the police without good reason. The same proportion claim they have been stopped in their cars. One in five says he has been searched unnecessarily; and one in six says that his car was searched for no good reason. The members of an interracial couple, particularly a Negro man accompanying a white woman, are perhaps the most vulnerable to harassment.

What citizens regard as police brutality many policemen consider necessary for law enforcement. While degrading epithets and abusive language may no longer be considered proper by either police commanders or citizens, they often disagree about other practices related to law enforcement. For example, although many citizens see "stop and question" or "stop and frisk" procedures as harassment, police commanders usually regard them merely as "aggressive prevention" to curb crime.

The nub of the police-brutality issue seems to lie in police use of physical force. By law, the police have the right to use such force if necessary to make an arrest, to keep the peace, or to maintain public order. But just how much force is necessary or proper?

This was the crucial problem we attempted to answer by placing observers in the patrol cars and in the precincts. Our 36 observers, divided equally between Chicago, Boston, and Washington, were responsible for reporting the details of all situations where police used physical force against a citizen. To ensure the observation of a large number of encounters, two high-crime police precincts were monitored in Boston and Chicago; four in Washington. At least one precinct was composed of primarily Negro residents, another primarily of whites. Where possible, we also tried to select precincts with considerable variation in social-class composition. Given the criterion of a high-crime rate, however, people of low socio-economic status predominated in most of the areas surveyed.

The law fails to provide simple rules about what—and how much—force that policemen can properly use. The American Bar Foundation's study *Arrest*, by Wayne La Fave, put the matter rather well, stating that the courts of all states would undoubtedly agree that in making an arrest a policeman should use only that amount of force he reasonably believes necessary. But La Fave also pointed out that there is no agreement on the question of when it is better to let the suspect escape than to employ "deadly" force.

Even in those states where the use of deadly force is limited by law, the kinds of physical force a policeman may use are not clearly defined. No kind of force is categorically denied a policeman, since he is always permitted to use deadly force in self-defense.

This right to protect himself often leads the policeman to argue self-defense whenever he uses force. We found that many policemen, whether or not the facts justify it, regularly follow their use of force with the charge that the citizen was assaulting a policeman or resisting arrest. Our observers also found that some policemen even carry pistols and knives that they have confiscated while searching citizens; they carry them so they may be placed at a scene should it be necessary to establish a case of self-defense.

Of course, not all cases of force involve the use of *unnecessary* force. Each instance of force reported by our observers was examined and judged to be either necessary or unnecessary. Cases involving simple restraint—holding a man by the arm—were deliberately excluded from consideration, even though a policeman's right to do so can, in many instances, be challenged. In judging when police force is "unwarranted," "unreasonable," or "undue," we rather deliberately selected only those cases in which a policeman struck the citizen with his hands, fist, feet, or body, or where he used a weapon of some kind—such as a nightstick or a pistol. In these cases, had the policeman been found to have used physical force improperly, he could have been arrested on complaint and, like any other citizen, charged with a simple or aggravated assault. A physical assault on a citizen was judged to be "improper" or "unnecessary" only if force was used in one or more of the following ways:

■ If a policeman physically assaulted a citizen and then failed to make an arrest; proper use involves an arrest.

■ If the citizen being arrested did not, by word or deed, resist the policeman; force should be used only if it is necessary to make the arrest.

■ If the policeman, even though there was resistance to the arrest, could easily have restrained the citizen in other ways.

■ If a large number of policemen were present and could have assisted in subduing the citizen in the station, in lockup, and in the interrogation rooms.

■ If an offender was handcuffed and made no attempt to flee or offer violent resistance.

■ If the citizen resisted arrest, but the use of force continued even after the citizen was subdued.

In the seven-week period, we found 37 cases in which force was used improperly. In all, 44 citizens had been assaulted. In 15 of these cases, no one was arrested. Of these, 8 had offered no verbal or physical resistance whatsoever, while 7 had.

An arrest was made in 22 of the cases. In 13, force was exercised in the station house when at least four other policemen were present. In two cases, there was no verbal or physical resistance to the arrest, but force was still applied. In two other cases, the police applied force to a handcuffed offender in a field setting. And in five situations, the offender did resist arrest, but the policeman continued to use force even after he had been subdued.

Just how serious was the improper use of force in these 44 cases? Naturally there were differences in degree of injury. In about one-half of the cases, the citizen appeared little more than physically bruised; in three cases, the amount of force was so great that the citizen had to be hospitalized. Despite the fact that cases can easily be selected for their dramatic rather than their representative quality, I want to present a few to give a sense of what the observers saw and reported as undue use of force.

In the following two cases, the citizens offered no physical or verbal resistance, and the two white policemen made no arrest. It is the only instance in which the observers saw the same two policemen using force improperly more than once.

The police precinct in which these incidents occurred is typical of those found in some of our larger cities, where the patrolmen move routinely from gold coast to slum. There are little islands of the rich and poor, of old Americans and new, of recent migrants and old settlers. One moves from high-rise areas of middle- and upper-income whites through an area of the really old Americans—Indians—to an enclave of the recently arrived. The recently arrived are primarily those the policemen call "hillbillies" (migrants from Kentucky and Tennessee) and "porkchops" (Puerto Ricans). There are ethnic islands of Germans and Swedes. Although there is a small area where Negroes live, it is principally a precinct of whites. The police in the district are, with one exception, white.

On a Friday in the middle of July, the observer arrived for the 4 to 12 midnight watch. The beat car that had been randomly chosen carried two white patrolmen—one with 14 years of experience in the precinct, the other with three.

The watch began rather routinely as the policemen cruised the district. Their first radio dispatch came at about 5:30 P.M. They were told to investigate two drunks in a cemetery. On arriving they found two white men "sleeping one off." Without questioning the men, the older policeman began to search one of them, ripping his shirt and hitting him in the groin with a nightstick. The younger policeman, as he searched the second, ripped away the seat of his trousers, exposing his buttocks. The policemen then prodded the men toward the cemetery fence and forced them to climb it, laughing at the plight of the drunk with the exposed buttocks. As the drunks went over the fence, one policemen shouted, "I ought to run you fuckers in!" The other remarked to the observer, "Those assholes won't be back; a bunch of shitty winos."

Not long after they returned to their car, the policemen stopped a woman who had made a left turn improperly. She was treated very politely, and the younger policeman, who wrote the ticket, later commented to the observer, "Nice lady." At 7:30 they were dispatched to check a suspicious auto. After a quick check, the car was marked abandoned.

Shortly after a 30-minute break for a 7:30 "lunch," the two policemen received a dispatch to take a burglary report. Arriving at a slum walkup, the police entered a room where an obviously drunk white man in his late 40s insisted that someone had entered and stolen his food and liquor. He kept insisting that it had been taken and that he had been forced to borrow money to buy beer. The younger policeman, who took the report, kept harassing the man, alternating between mocking and badgering him rhetorical questions. "You say your name is Half-A-Wit [for Hathaway]? Do you sleep with niggers? How did you vote on the bond issue? Are you sure that's all that's missing? Are you a virgin yet?" The man responded to all of this with the seeming vagueness and joviality of the intoxicated, expressing gratitude for the policemen's help as they left. The older policeman remarked to the observer as they left, "Ain't drunks funny?"

For the next hour little happened, but as the two were moving across the precinct shortly after 10 P.M., a white man and a woman in their 50s flagged them down. Since they were obviously "substantial" middle-class citizens of the district, the policemen listened to their complaints that a Negro man was causing trouble inside the public-transport station from which they had just emerged. The woman said that he had sworn at her. The older policeman remarked, "What's a nigger doing up here? He should be down on Franklin Road!"

With that, they ran into the station and grabbed the Negro man who was inside. Without questioning him, they shoved him into a phone booth and began beating him with their fists and a flashlight. They also hit him in the groin. Then they dragged him out and kept him on his knees. He pleaded that he had just been released from a mental hospital that day and, begging not to be hit again, asked them to let him return to the hospital. One policeman said: "Don't you like us, nigger? I like to beat niggers and rip out their eyes." They took him outside to their patrol car. Then they decided to put him on a bus, telling him that he was returning to the hospital; they deliberately put him on a bus going in the opposite direction. Just before the Negro boarded the bus, he said, "You police just like to shoot and beat people." The first policeman replied, "Get moving, nigger, or I'll shoot you." The man was crying and bleeding as he was put on the bus. Leaving the scene, the younger policeman commented, "He won't be back."

For the rest of the evening, the two policemen kept looking for drunks and harassing any they found. They concluded the evening by being dispatched to an address where, they were told, a man was being held for the police. No one answered their knock. They left.

The station house has long been suspected of harboring questionable police practices. Interrogation-room procedures have been attacked, particularly because of the methods the police have used to get confessions. The drama of the confession in the interrogation room has been complete with bright lights and physical torture. Whether or not such practices have ever existed on the scale suggested by popular accounts, confessions in recent years, even by accounts of offenders, have rarely been accompanied by such high drama. But recently the interrogation room has come under fire again for its failure to protect the constitutional rights of the suspect to remain silent and to have legal counsel.

The police station, however, is more than just a series of cubicles called interrogation rooms. There are other rooms and usually a lockup as well. Many of these are also hidden from public view. It is not surprising, then, that one-third of all the observations of the undue use of force occurred within the station.

In any station there normally are several policemen present who should be able to deal with almost any situation requiring force that arises. In many of the situations that were observed, as many as seven and eight policemen were present, most of whom simply stood by and watched force being used. The custom among policemen, it appeared, is that you intervene only if a fellow policeman needs help, or if you have been personally offended or affronted by those involved.

Force is used unnecessarily at many different points and places in the station. The citizen who is not co-operative during the booking process may be pushed or shoved, have his handcuffs twisted with a nightstick, have his foot stomped, or be pulled by the hair. All of these practices were reported by policemen as ways of obtaining "cooperation." But it was clear that the booking could have been completed without any of this harassment.

The lockup was the scene of some of the most severe applications of force. Two of the three cases requiring hospitalization came about when an offender was "worked over" in the lockup. To be sure, the arrested are not always cooperative when they get in the lockup, and force may be necessary to place them in a cell. But the amount of force observed hardly seemed necessary.

One evening an observer was present in the lockup when two white policemen came in with a white man. The suspect had been handcuffed and brought to the station because he had proved obstreperous after being arrested for a traffic violation. Apparently he had been drinking. While waiting in the lockup, the man began to urinate on the floor. In response, the policemen began to beat the man. They jumped him, knocked him down, and beat his head against the concrete floor. He required emergency treatment at a nearby hospital.

At times a policeman may be involved in a kind of escalation of force. Using force appropriately for an arrest in the field seemingly sets the stage for its later use, improperly, in the station. The following case illustrates how such a situation may develop:

Within a large city's high-crime rate precinct, occupied mostly by Negroes, the police responded to an "officer in trouble" call. It is difficult to imagine a call that brings a more immediate response, so a large number of police cars immediately converged at an intersection of a busy public street where a bus had been stopped. Near the bus, a white policeman was holding two young Negroes at gun point. The policeman reported that he had responded to a summons from the white bus-driver complaining that the boys had refused to pay their fares and had used obscene language. The policeman also reported that the boys swore at him, and one swung at him while the other drew a screwdriver and started toward him. At that point, he said, he drew his pistol.

The policemen placed one of the offenders in handcuffs and began to transport both of them to the station. While driving to the station, the driver of one
car noted that the other policeman, transporting the
other boy, was struggling with him. The first policeman stopped and entered the other patrol car. The
observer reported that he kept hitting the boy who
was handcuffed until the boy appeared completely subdued. The boy kept saying, "You don't have any right
to beat me. I don't care if you kill me."

After the policemen got the offenders to the station,
although the boys no longer resisted them, the police
began to beat them while they were handcuffed in an
interrogation room. One of the boys hollered: "You
can't beat me like this! I'm only a kid, and my hands
are tied." Later one of the policemen commented to
the observer: "On the street you can't beat them. But
when you get to the station, you can instill some respect in them."

Cases where the offender resists an arrest provide
perhaps the most difficulty in judging the legitimacy
of the force applied. An encounter that began as a
dispatch to a disturbance at a private residence was
one case about which there could be honest difference
in judgment. On arrival, the policemen—one white,
the other Negro—met a white woman who claimed
that her husband, who was in the back yard and drunk,
had beaten her. She asked the policemen to "take him
in." The observer reported that the police found the
man in the house. When they attempted to take him,
he resisted by placing his hands between the door
jamb. Both policemen then grabbed him. The Negro
policeman said, "We're going to have trouble, so let's

finish it right here." He grabbed the offender and knocked him down. Both policemen then wrestled with the man, handcuffed him, and took him to the station. As they did so, one of the policemen remarked, "These sons of bitches want to fight, so you have to break them quick."

The reader, as well as most police administrators, may be skeptical about reports that policemen used force in the presence of observers. Indeed, one police administrator, indignant over reports of undue use of force in his department, seemed more concerned that the policemen had permitted themselves to be observed behaving improperly than he was about their improper behavior. When demanding to know the names of the policemen who had used force improperly so he could discharge them—a demand we could not meet, since we were bound to protect our sources of information —he remarked, "Any officer who is stupid enough to behave that way in the presence of outsiders deserves to be fired."

There were and are a number of reasons why our observers were able to see policemen behaving improperly. We entered each department with the full cooperation of the top administrators. So far as the men in the line were concerned, our chief interest was in how citizens behave toward the police, a main object of our study. Many policemen, given their strong feelings against citizens, fail to see that their own behavior is equally open to observation. Furthermore, our observers are trained to fit into a role of trust— one that is genuine, since most observers are actually sympathetic to the plight of the policeman, if not to his behavior.

Finally, and this is a fact all too easily forgotten,

people cannot change their behavior in the presence of others as easily as many think. This is particularly true when people become deeply involved in certain situations. The policeman not only comes to "trust" the observer in the law-enforcement situation—regarding him as a source of additional help if necessary—but, when he becomes involved in a dispute with a citizen, he easily forgets that an observer is present. Partly because he does not know what else to do, in such situations the policeman behaves "normally." But should one cling to the notion that most policemen modify their behavior in the presence of outsiders, one is left with the uncomfortable conclusion that our cases represent a minimal picture of actual misbehavior.

Superficially it might seem that the use of an excessive amount of force against citizens is low. In only 37 of 3826 encounters observed did the police use undue force. Of the 4604 white citizens in these encounters, 27 experienced an excessive amount of force —a rate of 5.9 for every 1000 citizens involved. The comparable rate for 5960 Negroes, of whom 17 experienced an excessive amount of force, is 2.8. Thus, whether one considers these rates high or low, the fact is that the *rate of excessive force for all white citizens in encounters with the police is twice that for Negro citizens.*

A rate depends, however, upon selecting a population that is logically the target of force. What we have just given is a rate for *all* citizens involved in encounters with the police. But many of these citizens are not logical targets of force. Many, for example, simply call the police to complain about crimes against themselves or their property. And others are merely witnesses to crimes.

The more logical target population consists of citizens whom the police allege to be offenders—a population of suspects. In our study, there were 643 white suspects, 27 of whom experienced undue use of force. This yields an abuse rate of 41.9 per 1000 white suspects. The comparable rate for 751 Negro suspects, of whom 17 experienced undue use of force, is 22.6 per 1000. If one accepts these rates as reasonably reliable estimates of the undue force against suspects, then there should be little doubt that in major metropolitan areas the sort of behavior commonly called "police brutality" is far from rare.

Popular impression casts police brutality as a racial matter—white police mistreating Negro citizens. The fact is that white suspects are more liable to being treated improperly by the police than Negro suspects are. This, however, should not be confused with the chances a citizen takes of being mistreated. In two of the cities we studied, Negroes are a minority. The chances, then, that any Negro has of being treated improperly are, perhaps, more nearly comparable to that for whites. If the rates are comparable, then one might say that the application of force unnecessarily by the police operates without respect to the race of an offender.

Many people believe that the race of the policeman must affect his use of force, particularly since many white policemen express prejudice against Negroes. Our own work shows that in the police precincts made up largely of Negro citizens, over three-fourths of the policemen express prejudice against Negroes. Only 1 percent express sympathetic attitudes. But as sociologists and social psychologists have often shown, prejudice and attitudes do not necessarily carry over into discriminatory actions.

Our findings show that there is little difference between the rate of force used by white and by Negro policemen. Of the 54 policemen observed using too much force, 45 were white and 9 were Negro. For every 100 white policemen, 8.7 will use force; for every 100 Negro policemen, 9.8 will. What this really means, though, is that about one in every 10 policemen in high-crime rate areas of cities sometimes uses force unnecessarily.

Yet, one may ask, doesn't prejudice enter into the use of force? Didn't some of the policemen who were observed utter prejudiced statements toward Negroes and other minority-group members? Of course they did. But the question of whether it was their prejudice or some other factor that motivated them to mistreat Negroes is not so easily answered.

Still, even though our figures show that a white suspect is more liable to encounter violence, one may ask whether white policemen victimize Negroes more than whites. We found, for the most part, that they do not. Policemen, both Negro and white, are most likely to exercise force against members of their *own* race:

—67 percent of the citizens victimized by white policemen were white.

—71 percent of the citizens victimized by Negro policemen were Negro.

To interpret these statistics correctly, however, one should take into account the differences in opportunity policemen have to use force against members of their own and other races. Negro policemen, in the three cities we studied, were far *less* likely to police white citizens than white policemen were to police Negroes. Negro policemen usually policed other Negroes, while white policemen policed both whites and Negroes about equally. In total numbers, then, more white policemen than Negro policemen used force against Negroes. But this is explained by the fact that whites make up 85 percent of the police force, and more than 50 percent of all policemen policing Negroes.

Though no precise estimates are possible, the facts just given suggest that white policemen, even though they are prejudiced toward Negroes, do not discriminate against Negroes in the excessive use of force. The use of force by the police is more readily explained by police culture than it is by the policeman's race. Indeed, in the few cases where we observed a Negro policeman using unnecessary force against white citizens, there was no evidence that he did so because of his race.

The disparity between our findings and the public's sense that Negroes are the main victims of police brutality can easily be resolved if one asks how the public becomes aware of the police misusing force.

Fifty years ago, the immigrants to our cities—Eastern and Southern Europeans such as the Poles and the Italians—complained about police brutality. Today the new immigrants to our cities—mostly Negroes from the rural South—raise their voices through the civil-rights movement, through black-nationalist and other race-conscious organizations. There is no comparable voice for white citizens since, except for the Puerto

Ricans, they now lack the nationality organizations that were once formed to promote and protect the interests of their immigrant forbears.

Although policemen do not seem to select their victims according to race, two facts stand out. All victims were offenders, and all were from the lower class. Concentrating as we did on high-crime rate areas of cities, we do not have a representative sample of residents in any city. Nonetheless, we observed a sizable minority of middle- and upper-status citizens, some of whom were offenders. But since no middle- or upper-class offender, white or Negro, was the victim of an excessive amount of force, it appears that the lower class bears the brunt of victimization by the police.

The most likely victim of excessive force is a lower-class man of either race. No white woman and only two Negro women were victimized. The difference between the risk assumed by white and by Negro women can be accounted for by the fact that far more Negro women are processed as suspects or offenders.

Whether or not a policeman uses force unnecessarily depends upon the social setting in which the encounter takes place. Of the 37 instances of excessive force, 37 percent took place in police-controlled settings, such as the patrol car or the precinct station. Public places, usually streets, accounted for 41 percent, and 16 percent took place in a private residence. The remaining 6 percent occurred in commercial settings. This is not, of course, a random sample of settings where the police encounter suspects.

What is most obvious, and most disturbing, is that the police are very likely to use force in settings that they control. Although only 18 percent of all situations involving suspects ever ended up at the station house, 32 percent of all situations where an excessive amount of force was used took place in the police station.

No one who accepts the fact that the police sometimes use an excessive amount of force should be surprised by our finding that they often select their own turf. What should be apparent to the nation's police administrators, however, is that these settings are under their command and control. Controlling the police in the field, where the policeman is away from direct supervision, is understandably difficult. But the station house is the police administrator's domain. The fact that one in three instances of excessive force took place in settings that can be directly controlled should cause concern among police officials.

The presence of citizens who might serve as witnesses against a policeman should deter him from undue use of force. Indeed, procedures for the review of police conduct are based on the presumption that one can get this kind of testimony. Otherwise, one is left simply with a citizen complaint and contrary testimony by the policeman—a situation in which it is very difficult to prove the citizen's allegation.

In most situations involving the use of excessive force, there were witnesses. In our 37 cases, there were bystanders present three-fourths of the time. But in only one situation did the group present sympathize with the citizen and threaten to report the policeman. A complaint was filed on that incident—the only one of the 37 observed instances of undue force in which a formal complaint was filed.

All in all, the situations where excessive force was used were devoid of bystanders who did not have a stake in being "against" the offender. Generally, they were fellow policemen, or fellow offenders whose truthfulness could be easily challenged. When a policeman uses undue force, then, he usually does not risk a complaint against himself or testimony from witnesses who favor the complainant against the policeman. This, as much as anything, probably accounts for the low rate of formal complaints against policemen who use force unnecessarily.

A striking fact is that in more than one-half of all instances of undue coercion, at least one other policeman was present who did not participate in the use of force. This shows that, for the most part, the police do not restrain their fellow policemen. On the contrary, there were times when their very presence encouraged the use of force. One man brought into the lockup for threatening a policeman with a pistol was so severely beaten by this policeman that he required hospitalization. During the beating, some fellow policemen propped the man up, while others shouted encouragement. Though the official police code does not legitimate this practice, police culture does.

Now, are there characteristics of the offender or his behavior that precipitate the use of excessive force by the police? Superficially, yes. Almost one-half of the cases involved open defiance of police authority (39 percent) or resisting arrest (9 percent). Open defiance of police authority, however, is what the policeman defines as *his* authority, not necessarily "official" authority. Indeed in 40 percent of the cases that the police considered open defiance, the policeman never executed an arrest—a somewhat surprising fact for those who assume that policemen generally "cover" improper use of force with a "bona-fide" arrest and a charge of resisting arrest.

But it is still of interest to know what a policeman *sees* as defiance. Often he seems threatened by a simple refusal to acquiesce to his own authority. A policeman beat a handcuffed offender because, when told to sit, the offender did not sit down. One Negro woman was soundly slapped for her refusal to approach the police car and identify herself.

Important as a threat to his authority may appear to the policeman, there were many more of these instances in which the policeman did *not* respond with the use of force. The important issue seems to be whether the policeman manages to assert his authority despite the threat to it. I suspect that policemen are more likely to respond with excessive force when they define the situation as one in which there remains a question as to who is "in charge."

Similarly, some evidence indicates that harassment of deviants plays a role in the undue use of force. Incidents involving drunks made up 27 percent of all incidents of improper use of force; an additional 5 percent involved homosexuals or narcotics users. Since deviants generally remain silent victims to avoid public exposure of their deviance, they are particularly susceptible to the use of excessive force.

It is clear, though, that the police encounter many situations involving deviants where no force is used. Generally they respond to them routinely. What is surprising, then, is that the police do not mistreat deviants more than they do. The explanation may lie in the kind of relationships the police have with deviants. Many are valuable to the police because they serve as informers. To mistreat them severely would be to cut off a major source of police intelligence. At the same time, deviants are easily controlled by harassment.

Clearly, we have seen that police mistreatment of citizens exists. It is, however, on the increase?

Citizen complaints against the police are common, and allegations that the police use force improperly are frequent. There is evidence that physical brutality exists today. But there is also evidence, from the history of our cities, that the police have long engaged in the use of unnecessary physical force. No one can say with confidence whether there is more or less of it today than there was at the turn of the century.

What we lack is evidence that would permit us to calculate comparative rates of police misuse of force for different periods of American history. Only recently have we begun to count and report the volume of complaints against the police. And the research reported in this article represents the only attempt to estimate the amount of police mistreatment by actual observation of what the police do to citizens.

Police chiefs are notoriously reluctant to disclose information that would allow us to assess the nature and volume of complaints against the police. Only a few departments have begun to report something about citizen complaints. And these give us very little information.

Consider, for example, the 1966 Annual Report released by the New Orleans Police Department. It tells us that there were 208 cases of "alleged police misconduct on which action was taken." It fails to tell us whether there were any allegations that are *not* included among these cases. Are these all the allegations that came to the attention of the department? Or are they only those the department chose to review as "police disciplinary matters"? Of the 208 cases the department considered "disciplinary matters," the report tells us that no disciplinary action was taken in 106 cases. There were 11 cases that resulted in 14 dismissals; 56 cases that resulted in 72 suspensions, fines, or loss of days; and 35 cases involving 52 written or verbal "reprimands" or "cautionings."

The failure of the report to tell us the charge against the policeman is a significant omission. We cannot tell how many of these allegations involved improper use of force, how many involved verbal abuse or harassment, how many involved police felonies or misdemeanors, and so on. In such reports, the defensive posture of the nation's police departments is all too apparent. Although the 1966 report of the New Orleans Police Department tells us much about what the police allege were the felonies and misdemeanors by citizens of New Orleans, it tells us nothing about what citizens allege was misconduct by the police!

Many responsible people believe that the use of physical brutality by the police is on the wane. They point to the fact that, at least outside the South, there are more reports of other forms of police mistreatment of citizens than reports of undue physical coercion. They also suggest that third-degree interrogations and curbstone justice with the nightstick are less common. It does not seem unreasonable, then, to assume that police practices that degrade a citizen's status or that harass him and restrict his freedom are more common than police misuse of force. But that may have always been so.

Whether or not the policeman's "sense of justice" and his use of unnecessary force have changed remains an open question. Forms may change while practices go on. To move misuse from the street to the station house, or from the interrogation room to the lockup, changes the place but not the practice itself.

Our ignorance of just what goes on between police and citizens poses one of the central issues in policing today: How can we make the police accountable to the citizenry in a democratic society and yet not hamstring them in their legitimate pursuit of law and order? There are no simple answers.

Police departments are organizations that process people. All people-processing organizations face certain common problems. But the police administrator faces a problem in controlling practice with clients that is not found in most other organizations. The problem is that police contact with citizens occurs in the community, where direct supervision is not possible. Assuming our unwillingness to spend resources for almost one-to-one supervision, the problem for the police commander is to make policemen behave properly when they are not under direct supervision. He also faces the problem of making them behave properly in the station house as well.

Historically, we have found but one way—apart from supervision—that deals with this problem. That solution is professionalization of workers. Perhaps only through the professionalization of the police can we hope to solve the problem of police malpractice.

But lest anyone optimistically assume that professionalization will eliminate police malpractice altogether, we should keep in mind that problems of malpractice also occur regularly in both law and medicine.

July/August 1968

Crime, Victims, and the Police

PHILIP H. ENNIS

"A skid row drunk lying in a gutter is crime. So is the killing of an unfaithful wife. A Cosa Nostra conspiracy to bribe public officials is crime. So is a strong-arm robbery...." So states the report of the President's Commission on Law Enforcement and Administration of Justice, commonly known as the Crime Commission report, in pointing out the diversity of crime. Our recent investigation at Chicago's National Opinion Research Center reveals that Americans are also frequent prey to incidents which may not fall firmly within the jurisdiction of criminal law, but which still leave the ordinary citizen with a strong sense of victimization—consumer frauds, landlord-tenant violations, and injury or property damage due to someone else's negligent driving.

With the aid of a new research method for estimating national crime rates the Crime Commission study has now confirmed what many have claimed all along—that the rates

85

for a wide range of personal crimes and property offenses are considerably higher than previous figures would indicate. Traditional studies have relied on the police blotter for information. The present research, devised and carried out by the National Opinion Research Center (NORC), tried a survey approach instead. Taking a random sample of 10,000 households during the summer of 1965, we asked people what crimes had been committed against them during the preceding year. The results—roughly 2,100 verified incidents—indicated that as many as half of the people interviewed were victims of offenses which they did not report to the police.

This finding raised several questions. How much did this very high incidence of unreported offenses alter the picture presented by the standard measures, notably the FBI's Uniform Crime Reports (UCR) index, based only on reported incidents? What was the situation with minor offenses, those not considered in the UCR index? What sorts of crimes tended to go unreported? And why did so many victims fail to contact the authorities? These were some of the issues we attempted to probe.

More than 20 percent of the households surveyed were criminally victimized during the preceding year. This figure includes about *twice as much* major crime as reported by the UCR index. The incidence of minor crimes—simple assaults, petty larcenies, malicious mischiefs, frauds, and so on —is even greater. According to our research, these are at least twice as frequent as major crimes. The UCR index includes seven major crimes, so the proliferation of petty offenses not taken into account by the index makes the discrepancy between that index and the real crime picture even greater than a consideration of major offenses alone would indicate.

Table I compares our figures with the UCR rates for the

seven major crimes upon which the index is based—homicide, forcible rape, robbery, aggravated assault, burglary, larceny (over $50), and auto theft. The homicide rate projected by the survey is very close to the UCR rate—not surprising since murder is the crime most likely to be discovered and reported.

TABLE I—ESTIMATED RATES OF
MAJOR CRIMES: 1965-1966

Crime	NORC sample: estimated rate per 100,000	Uniform Crime Reports, 1965: individual or residential rates per 100,000
Homicide	3.0	5.1
Forcible rape	42.5	11.6
Robbery	94.0	61.4*
Aggravated assault	218.3	106.6
Burglary	949.1	296.6*
Larceny ($50+)	606.5	267.4*
Car theft	206.2	226.0†
Total	2,119.6	974.7

* The 1965 Uniform Crime Reports show for burglary and larcenies the number of residential and individual crimes. The overall rate per 100,000 population is therefore reduced by the proportion of these crimes that occurred to individuals. Since all robberies to individuals were included in the NORC sample regardless of whether the victim was acting as an individual or as part of an organization, the *total* UCR figure was used for comparison.

† The reduction of the UCR auto theft rate by 10 percent is based on the figures of the Automobile Manufacturers Association, showing that 10 percent of all cars are owned by leasing-rental agencies and private and governmental fleets. The Chicago Police Department's auto theft personnel confirmed that about 7-10 percent of stolen cars recovered were from fleet, rental, and other non-individually owned sources.

The survey estimate of the car theft rate is puzzlingly low. This could be because people report their cars "stolen" to the police and then find that they themselves have "misplaced" the car or that someone else has merely "borrowed" it. They may either forget the incident when interviewed or be too embarrassed to mention it. The relatively high rate of auto thefts reported to the police confirms other studies which show people are more likely to notify the police in this case than they are if they are victims of most other crimes. It may also indicate that people think the police can or will do more about a car theft than about many other offenses.

The startling frequency of reported forcible rape, four times that of the UCR index, underscores the peculiar nature of this crime. It occurs very often among people who know each other—at the extreme, estranged husband and wife—and there appears to be some stigma attached to the victim. Yet among the cases discovered in the survey, too few to be statistically reliable, most were reported to the police. Do the police tend to downgrade the offense into an assault or a minor sex case or put it into some miscellaneous category? This is a well-known practice for certain other kinds of crime.

To what extent is crime concentrated in the urban environment? To what extent are there regional differences in crime rates? And to what extent are the poor, and especially Negroes, more or less likely to be victims of crime? Behind these questions lie alternative remedial measures, measures which range from city planning and antipoverty programs to the training and organization of police departments and the allocation of their resources throughout the nation.

The NORC findings presented in Figure I give an overview of the crime rates for central cities in metropolitan areas, for their suburban environs, and for nonmetropolitan areas in the four main regions of the country. The chart shows the crime rate (per 100,000 population) for serious crimes against the person (homicide, rape, robbery, and

Figure 1—

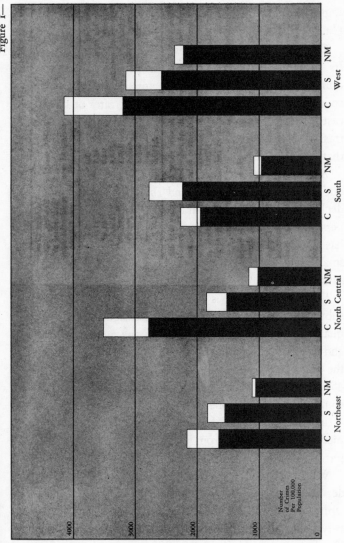

REGIONAL CRIME RATES BY TYPE OF COMMUNITY

C = Central cities   S = Suburban environs   NM = Nonmetropolitan areas

☐ Crimes against property   ■ Crimes against the person

aggravated assault) and serious crimes against property (burglary, larceny over $50, and vehicle theft).

The myth of the wild West is borne out by our figures. Its present crime rate, for both property and personal crimes, is higher than that of any other region of the country. The West has almost twice the rates of the Northeast for all three types of communities. The South, in contrast, does not appear to have the high rate of violent crime that is sometimes alleged.

As one moves from the central city to the suburbs and out into the smaller towns and rural areas, the crime rates decline, but much more drastically for crimes against the person than for property crimes. The metropolitan center has a violent crime rate about *five times* as high as the smaller city and rural areas, but a property crime rate only *twice* as high.

Evidently the city is a more dangerous place than the suburbs or a small town. Yet these figures require some qualification: About 40 percent of the aggravated assaults and rapes (constituting most of the serious crimes against the person) take place *within* the victim's home; and about 45 percent of all the serious crimes against the person are committed by someone familiar to the victim. Random "crime in the streets" by strangers is clearly *not* the main picture that emerges from these figures, even in the urban setting.

Who are the victims? Among lower income groups (under $6,000 per year) Negroes are almost twice as likely as whites to be victims of serious crimes of violence but only very slightly more likely to be victims of property crimes. Our figures show that, per 100,000 population, an estimated 748 low-income Negroes per year will be victims of criminal violence and 1,927 victims of property offenses, whereas the numbers for whites in the same income bracket are

402 and 1,829. The situation is exactly reversed for upper income groups. The wealthier Negro is not much more likely than the white to be a victim of a violent crime, but he is considerably more likely to have property stolen. His chances of losing property are 3,024 in 100,000, whereas the figure is only 1,765 for whites in the same income bracket. Burglary is the most common property crime against more affluent Negroes. The implication is that ghetto neighborhoods in which poor and richer Negroes live side by side make the latter more valuable to property losses than are higher income whites, who can live in more economically homogeneous areas.

Despite the fact then that per capita offense rates are generally acknowledged to be higher among Negroes than among whites, the incidence of whites being victimized by Negroes—an image frequently conjured up by the specter of "crime in the streets"—is relatively infrequent. Negroes tend instead to commit offenses against members of their own race. The same is true of whites. Further, to the extent that crime is interracial at all, Negroes are more likely to be victims of white offenders than vice versa. Our figures show that only 12 percent of the offenses against whites in our sample were committed by nonwhites, whereas 19 percent of the nonwhite victims reported that the persons who committed offenses against them were white.

What happens when a person is victimized? How often are law enforcement and judicial authorities involved? What changes occur in the victim's attitude and behavior as a result of the incident?

If the "right thing" to do is to call the police when you have been a victim of a crime, and there is considerable pressure to do just that, why is it that half the victimizations were not reported to the police?

The more serious the crime, the more likely it is to be

reported: 65 percent of the aggravated assaults in our sample were reported to the police, but only 46 percent of the simple assaults; 60 percent of the grand larcenies, but only 37 percent of the petty larcenies. Insurance recovery also appears to play a role in the very high rate of reported auto thefts (89 percent) and reported victimizations that are the result of automobile negligence (71 percent). Victims of offenses at the border of the criminal law apparently do not think the police should be involved. Only 10 percent of the consumer fraud victims called the police, whereas 26 percent of the ordinary fraud victims (mainly those of bad checks) did so.

Those victims who said they did not notify the police were asked why. Their reasons fell into four fairly distinct categories. The first was the belief that the incident was not a police matter. These victims (34 percent) did not want the offender to be harmed by the police or thought that the incident was a private, not a criminal, affair. Two percent of the nonreporting victims feared reprisal, either physically from the offender's friends or economically from cancellation of or increases in rates of insurance. Nine percent did not want to take the time or trouble to get involved with the police, did not know whether they should call the police, or were too confused to do so. Finally, a substantial 55 percent of the nonreporting victims failed to notify the authorities because of their attitudes toward police effectiveness. These people believed the police could not do anything about the incident, would not catch the offenders, or would not want to be bothered.

The distribution of these four types of reasons for failure to notify police varies by type of crime and by the social characteristics of the victim, but two points are clear. First, there is strong resistance to invoking the law enforcement process even in matters that are clearly criminal. Second, there is considerable skepticism as to the effectiveness of police action.

A clue to this skepticism lies in the events which follow a call to the police. All the victims who reported an offense were asked how the police reacted and how far the case proceeded up the judicial ladder—arrest, trial, sentencing, and so forth. We have simplified the process into six stages:

■ Given a "real" victimization, the police were or were not notified.

■ Once notified, the police either came to the scene of the victimization (or in some other way acknowledged the event) or failed to do so.

■ Once they arrived, the police did or did not regard the incident as a crime.

■ Regarding the matter as a crime, the police did or did not make an arrest.

■ Once an arrest was made, there was or was not a trial (including plea of guilty).

■ The outcome of the trial was to free the suspect (or punish him "too leniently") or to find him guilty and give him the "proper" punishment.

Figure II shows the tremendous attrition as the cases proceed from the bottom of the "iceberg," the initial victimization, to the top, the trial and sentencing. Failure of the police to heed a call and their rejection of the incident as a crime account for a large proportion of this attrition. Also noteworthy are the low arrest and trial rates. Once the offender is brought to trial, however, the outcome appears more balanced. About half the offenders were treated too leniently in the victim's view, but the other half were convicted and given "proper" punishment.

How do the victims feel about this truncated legal process? Do they feel that the situation is their own fault and

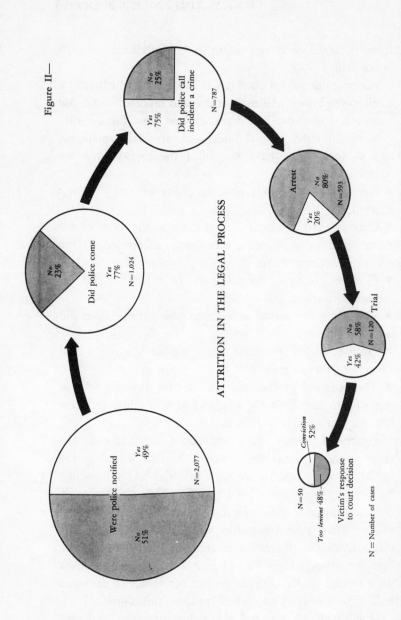

Figure II—

ATTRITION IN THE LEGAL PROCESS

Were police notified
Yes 49%
No 51%
N=2,077

Did police come
Yes 77%
No 23%
N=1,024

Did police call incident a crime
Yes 75%
No 25%
N=787

Arrest
Yes 20%
No 80%
N=593

Trial
Yes 42%
No 58%
N=120

Victim's response to court decision
Conviction 52%
Too lenient 48%
N=50

N = Number of cases

accept it, or are they dissatisfied with the relatively frequent failure of the police to apprehend the offender? When the victims were asked their feelings about the outcome of the incident, only 18 percent said they were very satisfied; another 19 percent were somewhat satisfied; 24 percent were somewhat dissatisfied; and 35 percent were very dissatisfied (4 percent gave no answer).

The level of satisfaction was closely related to how far the case went judicially. (See Table II.) People who did not call the police at all were the most dissatisfied. If they called and the police did not come, about the same percentage were very dissatisfied; but peculiarly, there were more who reported that they were satisfied. An arrest lowered the dissatisfaction level, but the dramatic differences appeared when the offender was brought to trial. If he was acquitted or given too lenient a penalty (in the victim's view), dissatisfaction ran high; if he was convicted and given the "proper" penalty, the victim was generally quite pleased. This suggests that the ordinary citizen's sense of justice includes a vengeful element—a desire for punishment over and above monetary compensation for loss. Advocates of rehabilitation rather than retribution for criminals might well take such public sentiments into account.

Quite independent of the judicial outcome of the case is its impact on the daily life and feelings of the victim and his family. Slightly more than 40 percent of the victims reported increased suspicion and distrustfulness along with intensified personal and household security measures. It appears that it is the unpredictability of the event and the sense of invasion by strangers rather than the seriousness of the crime that engenders this mistrust. With these strong feelings and the frequent lack of knowledge about the identity of the offender, victimization may well

TABLE II—DEGREE OF SATISFACTION WITH OUTCOME OF OFFENSE

Disposition of case	Very satisfied	Somewhat satisfied	Somewhat dissatisfied	Very dissatisfied
No notification of police	13%	18%	28%	41%
Police did not respond to notification	22	22	18	38
Police did not consider incident a crime	24	26	24	26
Crime, but no arrest	20	23	27	30
Arrest, but no trial	33	21	22	24
Acquittal or too lenient penalty	17	13	26	44
Conviction and "proper" penalty	60	16	12	12

exacerbate existing prejudice against the groups typically blamed for social disorder and crime.

How does the public feel about the police? The survey asked all the crime victims and a comparably large sample of nonvictims a series of questions probing their attitudes on how well the local police do their job, how respectful they are toward the citizenry, and how honest they are. Items concerning the limits of police authority and exploring the functions of the police were also included.

Several conclusions emerged. Upper income groups are consistently more favorable in their evaluation of the police and are more in favor of augmenting their power than those with lower incomes. Negroes at all income levels show strong negative attitudes toward the police. (See Tables III and IV.)

Table III shows rather clearly that Negroes, regardless of income, estimate police effectiveness lower than whites do, with Negro women being even more critical than Negro men of the job the police are doing. Furthermore, Negroes show a smaller shift in attitude with increasing income than do whites, who are more favorable in their opinion of police effectiveness as their income rises.

TABLE III—POSITIVE OPINIONS ON
LOCAL POLICE EFFECTIVENESS

(Percentage who think police do an excellent or
good job in enforcing the law)

	White		Nonwhite	
Sex	Less than $6,000	$6,000 or more	Less than $6,000	$6,000 or more
Male	67%	72%	54%	56%
Female	66	74	39	43

Table IV shows that Negroes are also sharply more critical than whites are of police honesty. Here there are no income differences in attitude among white males. Women at higher income levels, both white and Negro, appear to be relatively less suspicious of police honesty. It is difficult to say how much these attitude differences are attributable to actual experience with police corruption and how much they express degrees of general hostility to the police. In either case the results indicate a more negative attitude toward the police among Negroes than among whites.

TABLE IV—OPINIONS ON THE HONESTY OF NEIGHBORHOOD POLICE

| | Males | | | |
| | White | | Nonwhite | |
Police are . . .	Less than $6,000	$6,000 or more	Less than $6,000	$6,000 or more
Almost all honest	65%	67%	33%	33%
Most honest, few corrupt	24	26	47	41
Almost all corrupt	3	1	9	19
Don't know	8	6	11	7

| | Females | | | |
| | White | | Nonwhite | |
Police are . . .	Less than $6,000	$6,000 or more	Less than $6,000	$6,000 or more
Almost all honest	57%	65%	24%	35%
Most honest, few corrupt	27	29	54	49
Almost all corrupt	2	0	10	4
Don't know	14	6	12	12

The next question probed a more personal attitude toward the police—their respectfulness toward "people like yourself." Almost 14 percent of the Negroes answered that it was "not so good." Less than 3 percent of the whites chose this response. This represents a much more critical attitude by Negroes than by whites, with hardly any differences by sex or income. There is some tendency, however, for very low income people of both races and sexes to feel that the police are not sufficiently respectful to them.

One further conclusion is more tentative. It appears that there is no *one* underlying attitude toward the police. The police have many and sometimes only slightly related jobs to do in society. For example, they have a role both in suppressing organized gambling and in maintaining civil order. Most people (73 percent) feel the police should stop gambling even though it brings a good deal of money into the community. A significant minority (21 percent) feel the police should act only on complaints, and only 2 percent said the police should not interfere with gambling at all. With respect to police control of demonstrations for civil and political rights, on the other hand, a slight majority (54 percent) say police should not interfere if the protests are peaceful; 40 percent say police should stop all demonstrations; and 3 percent feel demonstrations should be allowed under any and all circumstances. Negroes are much more permissive about demonstrations than whites, and somewhat more permissive about gambling. Among lower income Negroes there is a significant relation between permissiveness on gambling and a strong prodemonstration attitude. But whites show no such consistent attitudes on the two issues. They tend to favor police intervention in gambling but not in rights demonstrations.

A more dramatic example of discontinuities in attitudes toward police has to do with limitations on their power. A national cross-section of citizens was asked:

■ "Recently some cities have added civilian review boards to their police departments. Some people say such boards offer the public needed protection against the police, and others say these boards are unnecessary and would interfere with good police work and morale. In general, would you be in favor of civilian review boards or opposed to them?"

In favor _____ 45%

Opposed _____ 35

Don't know _____ 20

■ "Do you favor giving the police more power to question people, do you think they have enough power already, or would you like to see some of their power to question people curtailed?"

Police should have more power _____ 52%

Have enough power already _____ 43

Should curtail power _____ 5

■ "The police sometimes have a hard time deciding if there is enough evidence to arrest a suspect. In general, do you think it is better for them to risk arresting an innocent person rather than letting the criminal get away, or is it better for them to be really sure they are getting the right person before they make an arrest?"

Risk arresting innocent _____ 42%

Be really sure _____ 58

■ "The Supreme Court has recently ruled that in criminal cases the police may not question a suspect without his lawyer being present, unless the suspect agrees to be questioned without a lawyer. Are you in favor of this Supreme Court decision or opposed to it?"

In favor _____ 65%

Opposed _____ 35

The significance of these results is their lack of consensus. On none of the questions is there overwhelming agreement or disagreement. Opinions are split almost in half, with the exception that hardly anyone is in favor of curtailing present police powers. The advocates of extending police authority in questioning suspects are almost balanced by those who think the police have enough power to do their job. Further, there is lack of internal agreement on the specific facets of the question. Being in favor of a civilian review board does not necessarily make a person support the Supreme Court decision on interrogation of suspects. Nor does a preference for having the police risk arresting the innocent rather than letting a criminal go free strongly predict being in favor of granting more power to the police in questioning people.

It is not clear why attitudes toward the police are so scattered. Perhaps police power is too new an issue on the national scene to have its components hammered into a clear and cohesive whole. Local variations in police practices may also blur the situation. It appears we are only at the beginning of a long process of relocating the police in the political spectrum.

As the federal presence in local law enforcement enlarges, both the shape of crime and the nature of law enforcement itself will change. Accurate crime statistics will be essential in monitoring these changes and in evaluating the worth of new programs designed to protect the public from the growing threat of invasion and victimization by criminal acts.

June 1967

FURTHER READING SUGGESTED BY THE AUTHOR:

The Challenge of Crime in a Free Society (Washington, D.C.: United States Government Printing Office). A report by the President's Commission on Law Enforcement and Administration of Justice.

The American Jury by Harry Kalven, Jr. and Hans Zeisel (Boston: Little, Brown and Company, 1966).

Arrest edited by Wayne R. LaFave (Boston: Little, Brown and Company, 1965). The report of the American Bar Foundation's Survey of the Administration of Criminal Justice in the United States.

Sniping...
A New Pattern of Violence?

TERRY ANN KNOPF

On July 23, 1968, at 2:15 P.M., Cleveland's Mayor, Carl B. Stokes, who was in Washington, D.C., that day, made what he expected to be a routine telephone call to his office back home. He was told of information from military, F.B.I., and local police intelligence sources indicating that an armed uprising by black militants was scheduled to take place at 8 A.M. the next day. According to the reports, Ahmed Evans, a militant leader who headed a group called the Black Nationalists of New Libya, planned to drive to Detroit that night to secure automatic weapons. There were further reports that Evans' followers had already purchased bandoliers, ammunition pouches, and first-aid kits that same day. Simultaneous uprisings were reportedly being planned for Detroit, Pittsburgh, and Chicago.

At 6 P.M., in response to these reports, several unmarked police cars were assigned to the area of Evans' house. At about 8:20 P.M. a group of armed men, some of whom were wearing bandoliers of ammunition, emerged from the house. Almost at once, an intense gun battle broke out between the police and the armed men, lasting for roughly an hour. A second gun battle between the police and snipers broke out shortly after midnight about 40 blocks away. In the wake of these shoot-outs, sporadic looting and firebombing erupted and continued for several days. By the time the disorder was over, 16,400 National Guardsmen had been mobilized, at least nine persons had been killed (including three policemen), while the property damage was estimated at $1.5 million. Police listed most of their casualties as "shot by sniper."

Immediately, the Cleveland tragedy was described as a deliberate plot against the police and said to signal a new phase in the current course of racial conflict. *The Cleveland Press* (July 24, 1968) compared the violence in Cleveland to guerrilla activity in Saigon and noted: ". . . It didn't seem to be a Watts, or a Detroit, or a Newark. Or even a Hough of two years ago. No, this tragic night seemed to be part of a plan." Thomas A. Johnson writing in *The New York Times* (July 28, 1968) stated: ". . . It marks perhaps the first documented case in recent history of black, armed, and organized violence against the police."

As the notion that police were being "ambushed" took hold in the public's mind, many observers reporting on the events in Cleveland and similar confrontations in other cities, such as Gary, Peoria, Seattle, and York, Pennsylvania, emphasized that the outbreaks had several prominent features in common.

The first was the element of planning. Racial outbursts have traditionally been spontaneous affairs, without organization and without leadership. While no two disorders are similar in every respect, studies conducted in the past have indicated that a riot is a dynamic process that goes through stages of development. John P. Spiegel of Brandeis' Lemberg Center for the Study of Violence, has discerned four stages in the usual sort of rioting: the precipitating event, street confrontation, "Roman holiday," and seige. A sequence of stages is outlined in somewhat similar terms in the section of the Kerner Report on "the riot process." It is significant, however, that neither the Lemberg Center nor the Kerner Commission found any evidence of an organized plan or "conspiracy" in civil disorders prior to 1968. According to the Kerner Report: ". . . The Commission has found no evidence that all or any of the disorders or the incidents that led to them were planned or directed by any organization or group—international, national, or local."

Since the Cleveland shoot-out, however, many observers have suggested that civil disorders are beginning to take a new form, characterized by some degree of planning, organization, and leadership.

The second new feature discerned in many of 1968's summer outbreaks was the attacks on the police. In the past, much of the racial violence that occurred was directed at property rather than persons. Cars were stoned, stores were looted, business establishments were firebombed, and residences, in some instances, were damaged or destroyed. However, since the Cleveland gun battle, there have been suggestions that policemen have become the primary targets of violence. A rising curve of ambushes of the police was noted in the October 7, 1968 issue of the *U.S. News & World Report* which maintained that at least 8 policemen were killed and 47 wounded in such attacks last summer.

Finally, attacks on the police are now said to be *regularly* characterized by hit-and-run sniping. Using either home-made weapons or commercial and military weapons, such as automatics, bands of snipers are pictured initiating guerrilla warfare in our cities.

This view of the changing nature of racial violence can be found across a broad spectrum of the press, ranging from the moderately liberal *New York Times* to the miltantly rightist *American Opinion*. On August 3, 1968, *The New York Times* suggested in an editorial:

. . . The pattern in 1967 has not proved to be the pattern of 1968. Instead of violence almost haphazardly exploding, it has sometimes been deliberately planned. And while the 1967 disorders served to rip away false facades of racial progress and expose rusting junkyards of broken promises, the 1968 disorders also reveal a festering militancy that prompts some to resort to open warfare.

Shortly afterward (August 14, 1968), *Crime Control Digest,* a biweekly periodical read by many law-enforcement officials across the country, declared:

The pattern of civil disorders in 1968 has changed from the pattern that prevailed in 1967, and the elaborate U.S. Army, National Guard and police riot control program prepared to meet this year's "long hot summer" will have to be changed if this year's type of civil disturbance is to be prevented or controlled.

This year's riot tactics have featured sniping and hit-and-run attacks on the police, principally by Black Power extremists, but by teen-agers in an increasing number of instances. The type of crimes being committed by the teen-agers and the vast increase in their participation has already brought demands that they be tried and punished as adults.

On September 13, 1968, *Time* took note of an "ominous trend" in the country:

Violence as a form of Negro protest appears to be changing from the spontaneous combustion of a mob to the premeditated shoot-outs of a far-out few. Many battles have started with well-planned sniping at police.

Predictably, the November 1968 issue of *American Opinion* went beyond the other accounts by linking reported attacks on the police to a Communist plot:

The opening shots of the Communists' long-planned terror offensive against our local police were fired in Cleveland on the night of July 23, 1968, when the city's Glenville area rattled with the scream of automatic weapons. . . . What happened in Cleveland, alas, was only a beginning.

To further emphasize the point, a large headline crying "terrorism" was included on the cover of the November issue.

Despite its relative lack of objectivity, *American Opinion* is the only publication that has attempted to list sniping incidents. Twenty-five specific instances of attacks on police were cited in the November issue. Virtually every other publication claiming a change in the nature of racial violence pointing to the "scores of American cities" affected and the "many battles" between blacks and the police has confined itself to a few perfunctory examples as evidence. Even when a few examples have been offered, the reporters usually have not attempted to investigate and confirm them.

Without attempting an exhaustive survey, we at the Lemberg Center were able to collect local and national press clippings, as well as wire-service stories, that described 25 separate incidents of racial violence in July and

August of last summer. In all these stories, sniping was alleged to have taken place at some point or other in the fracas, and in most of them, the police were alleged to have been the primary targets of the sharpshooters. Often, too, the reports held that evidence had been found of planning on the part of "urban guerrillas," and at times it was claimed that the police had been deliberately ambushed. Needless to say, the specter of the Black Panthers haunts a number of the accounts. Throughout, one finds such phrases as these: "snipers hidden behind bushes . . . ," "isolated sniper fire . . . ," "scattered sniping directed at the police . . . ," "exchange of gunfire between snipers and police . . . ," "snipers atop buildings in the area. . . ." It is small wonder that the rewrite men at *Time* and other national magazines discerned a new and sinister pattern in the events of that summer. Small wonder that many concerned observers are convinced that the country's racial agony has entered a new phase of deliberate covert violence.

But how valid is this sometimes conspiratorial, sometimes apocalyptic view? What is the evidence for it, apart from these newspaper accounts?

Our assessment is based on an analysis of newspaper clippings, including a comparison of initial and subsequent reports, local and national press coverage, and on telephone interviews with high-ranking police officials. The selection of police officials was deliberate on our part. In the absence of city or state investigations of most of the incidents, police departments were found to be the best (and in many cases the only) source of information. Moreover, as the reported targets of sniping, police officials understandably had a direct interest in the subject.

Of course, the selection of this group did involve an element of risk. A tendency of some police officials to exaggerate and inflate sniping reports was thought to be unavoidable. We felt, though, that every group involved would have a certain bias and that in the absence of interviewing every important group in the cities, the views of police officials were potentially the most illuminating and therefore the most useful. Our interviews with them aimed at the following points: 1) evidence of planning; 2) the number of snipers; 3) the number of shots fired; 4) affiliation of the sniper or snipers with an organization; 5) statistical breakdowns of police and civilian casualties by sniping; and 6) press coverage of the incident.

As the press reports showed, a central feature in the scheme of those alleging a new pattern involves the notion of planning. Hypothesizing a local (if not national) conspiracy, observers have pictured black militants luring the police to predetermined spots where the policemen become the defenseless victims of an armed attack. No precipitating incident is involved in these cases except perhaps for a false citizen's call.

Despite this view, the information we gathered indicates that at least 17 out of the 25 disorders surveyed (about 70 percent) *did* begin with an identifiable precipitating event (such as an arrest seen by the black community as insulting or unjust) similar to those uncovered for "traditional" disorders. The figure of 70 percent is entirely consistent with the percentage of known precipitating incidents isolated by researchers at the Lemberg Center for past disorders (also about 70 percent).

In Gary, Indiana, the alleged sniping began shortly after two young members of a gang were arrested on charges of rape. In York, Pennsylvania, the violence began after a white man fired a shotgun from his apartment at some blacks on the street. Blacks were reportedly angered

upon learning that the police had failed to arrest the gun-
man. In Peoria, Illinois, police arrested a couple for creating a disturbance in a predominantly black housing-
project area. A group of young people then appeared on the
scene and began throwing missiles at the police. In Seattle,
Washington, a disturbance erupted shortly after a rally
was held to protest the arrest of two men at the local
Black Panther headquarters. Yet the disorders that followed
these incidents are among the most prominently mentioned as examples of planned violence.

Many of the precipitating events were tied to the actions of the police and in some instances they were what the
Kerner Commission has referred to as "tension-heightening
incidents," meaning that the incident (or the disorder itself) merely crystallized tensions already existing in the
community. Shortly before an outbreak in Harvey-Dixmoor, Illinois, on August 6–7, for example, a coroner's
jury had ruled that the fatal shooting by police of a
young, suspected car thief one month earlier was justifiable
homicide. It was the second time in four months that a
local policeman had shot a black youth. In Miami, the
rally held by blacks shortly before the violence erupted
coincided with the Republican National Convention being
held about 10 miles away. The crowd was reportedly disappointed when the Reverend Ralph Abernathy and basket-
ball star Wilt Chamberlain failed to appear as announced.
In addition, tensions had risen in recent months following
increased police canine patrols in the area. Although no
immediate precipitating incident was uncovered for the
outbreak at Jackson, Michigan on August 5, it is noteworthy that the disorder occurred in front of a Catholic-
sponsored center aimed at promoting better race relations,
and several weeks earlier, some 30 blacks had attempted

to take over the center in the name of "a black group run by black people."

Let us turn briefly to the eight disorders in which triggering events do not appear to have occurred. Despite the absence of such an incident in the Chicago Heights-East Chicago Heights disorder, Chief of Police Robert A. Stone (East Chicago Heights) and Captain Jack Ziegler (Chicago Heights) indicated that they had no evidence of planning and that the disorder was in all probability spontaneous. In particular, Chief Stone indicated that the participants were individuals rather than members of an organization. The same holds true for the "ambuscade" in Brooklyn, New York, which the district attorney said at the time was the work of the Black Panthers. Although no precipitating event was uncovered, R. Harcourt Dodds, Deputy Commissioner for Legal Matters in the New York City Police Department, indicated there was no evidence of planning by anyone or any group. In Jackson, Michigan, as previously noted, tensions in the community had increased in recent weeks prior to the August disorder over a controversial center which some members of the community thought they should control. Thus the absence of precipitating events in at least three cases does not appear to be significant, least of all as evidence of a deliberate conspiracy to kill.

An assessment of the other five cases is considerably more difficult. In Inkster, Michigan, where four nights of isolated sniper fire were reported in August, Chief of Police James L. Fyke did not identify any precipitating event with the disorder and indicated that the state planned to make a case for conspiracy at a forthcoming trial. On the grounds that the two disorders in his city were under police investigation, Lieutenant Norman H. Judd of the Los Angeles Police Department declined comment on possible triggering events. In San Francisco, Chief of Police Thomas J. Cahill said there was evidence of planning. He said that "a firebomb was ignited and the shots were fired as the police vehicle arrived at the scene."

This brings us to Cleveland and Ahmed Evans, the fifth case in this instance. Because of the dramatic nature of the events and the tremendous amount of attention they received in the national press, any findings concerning Cleveland are of utmost importance. It is significant, therefore, that more recent reports have revealed that the July bloodletting was something less than a planned uprising and that the situation at the time was considerably more complicated than indicated initially.

A series of articles appearing in *The New York Times* is instructive. At the time of the disorder, in an account by Thomas A. Johnson, entitled "This Was Real Revolution," *The New York Times* gave strong hints of a plot against the police: "Early indications here were that a small, angry band of Negro men decided to shoot it out with the police. . . ." The article dwelt upon past statements of Ahmed Evans predicting armed uprisings across the nation on May 9, 1967 (they never materialized), rumors of arms caches across the country, and the revolutionary talk of black militants. No mention was made of any precipitating event, nor was there any reference to "tension-heightening incidents" in the community at the time.

One month later, in early September, *The New York Times* published the results of its investigation of the disorder. The report was prepared by three newsmen, all of whom had covered the disorder earlier. Their findings shed new light on the case by suggesting that a series of tension-heightening factors were indeed present in the community at the time of the disorder. For one thing, Mayor Stokes attended a meeting with police officials several hours before the first outbreak and felt that the information about a planned uprising was "probably not correct." Ahmed Evans himself was seen, retrospectively, less as the mastermind of a plot than as just another militant. Anthony Ripley of *The New York Times* wrote of him: "Evans, a tall, former Army Ranger who had been dishonorably discharged after striking an officer, was not regarded as a leading black nationalist. He was an amateur astrologer, 40 years old, given more to angry speeches than to action." Numerous grievances in the community—particularly against the police—which had been overlooked at the time of the disorder, were cited later. For example, it was noted that there were only 165 blacks on a police force of more than 2,000 officers, and there was a deep resentment felt by blacks toward their treatment by the police. The reporters also turned up the fact that in 1966 an investigation committee had given a low professional rating to the police department.

Ahmed Evans himself had some more specific grievances, according to Thomas A. Johnson's follow-up article. He noted that Evans had arranged to rent a vacant tavern for the purpose of teaching the manufacture of African-style clothes and carvings to black youths but that the white landlady had changed her mind. He said that Evans had been further angered upon receiving an eviction order from his home. The Ripley article noted that, two hours before the shooting began, Evans said he had been asleep until his associates informed him that police surveillance cars had been stationed in the area. (Evans was accustomed to posting lookouts on top of buildings.) According to Evans, it was then that the group made the decision to arm.

Did the presence of the police in the area serve to trigger the gun battle that followed? What was the role of the civilian tow-truck driver wearing a police-like uniform? Did his hitching up an old pink Cadillac heighten tensions to the breaking point? Were intelligence reports of a plot in error? Why were arms so readily available to the group? What was the group's intention upon emerging from the house? These questions cannot be answered with any degree of absolute certainty. Nevertheless, it is significant that the earliest interpretations appearing in *The New York Times* were greatly modified by the subsequent articles revealing the complexities of the disorder and suggesting it may have been more spontaneous than planned. As Ripley wrote in his September 2 article:

> The Cleveland explosion has been called both an ambush of police and an armed uprising by Negroes. However, the weight of evidence indicates that it was closer to spontaneous combustion.

More recent developments on the controversial Cleveland case deserve mention also. On May 12, 1969, an all-white jury found Ahmed Evans guilty of seven counts of first-degree murder arising out of four slayings during the disorder last July. Evans was sentenced to die in the electric chair on September 22, 1969.

Then, on May 29, 1969, the National Commission on the Causes and Prevention of Violence authorized the release of a report entitled *Shoot-Out in Cleveland; Black Militants and the Police: July 23, 1968* by Louis H. Masotti and Jerome R. Corsi. The report was partially underwritten by the Lemberg Center. Its findings confirmed many of the results of *The Times* investigation and provided additional insights into the case.

Doubt was cast on prior intelligence reports that the Evans group had been assembling an arsenal of handguns and carbines, that Evans planned a trip to Detroit to secure weapons, and that simultaneous outbreaks in other northern cities were planned. ("The truth of these reports was questionable.") Further, it was revealed that these reports came from a single individual and that "other intelligence sources did not corroborate his story." In addition, the Commission report underscored certain provocative actions by the police:

It was glaringly evident that the police had established a stationary surveillance rather than a moving one. In fact, another surveillance car was facing Ahmed's apartment building from the opposite direction. . . . Both cars contained only white officers; both were in plain view of Ahmed's home. . . . Rightly or wrongly, Ahmed regarded the obvious presence of the surveillance cars over several hours' time as threatening.

The report stressed that "against theories of an ambush or well-planned conspiracy stands the evidence that on Tuesday evening [July 23, 1968] Ahmed was annoyed and apprehensive about the police surveillance."

The Times experience, together with the report of the National Commission on the Causes and Prevention of Violence, strongly suggest that the assumption that the Cleveland disorder was planned is as yet unproved.

It may be significant that 14 out of the 19 police officials who expressed a view on the matter could find no evidence of planning in the disorders in their respective cities. In another instance, the police official said the disorder was planned, but he could offer no evidence in support of his statement. If this and the Cleveland case are added, the number of outbreaks that do not appear to have been planned comes to at least 16 out of 19.

In their assertions that police are now the principal targets of snipers, some observers give the impression that there have been large numbers of police casualties. In most cases, the reports have not been explicit in stating figures. However, as mentioned earlier, *U.S. News & World Report* cited 8 police deaths and 47 police woundings this past summer. In order to assess these reports, we obtained from police officials a breakdown of police casualties as a result of gunfire.

What we learned was that a total of four policemen were killed and that each death was by gunfire. But three of these occurred in one city, Cleveland; the other was in Inkster, Michigan. In other words, in 23 out of 25 cases where sniping was originally reported, no policemen were killed.

Our total agreed with figures initially taken from local press reports. However, our count of four dead was only half the figure reported in *U.S. News & World Report.* We learned why when we found that the story appearing in that magazine originally came from an Associated Press "roundup," which said that eight policemen had been killed by gunfire since July 1, 1968. But four of these eight cases were in the nature of individual acts of purely criminal—and not racial—violence. On July 2, a Washington, D.C., policeman was killed when he tried to arrest a man on a robbery complaint. A Philadelphia policeman was killed July 15 while investigating a $59 streetcar robbery. On August 5, in San Antonio, a policeman was killed by a 14-year-old boy he had arrested. The youth was a Mexican-American who had been arrested on a drinking charge. And, in Detroit, a policeman was shot to death on August 5 following a domestic quarrel. The circumstances concerning these four cases in no way display the features of a "new pattern" of violence.

The question of how many police *injuries* came from sniper fire is more complicated. A total of 92 policemen were injured, accounting for 14 out of 25 cases. Almost half the injuries—44—came from gunfire. In some instances, our findings showed a downward revision of our earlier information. In Gary, for example, somebody reportedly took a shot at Police Chief James F. Hilton as he cruised the troubled area shortly after the disturbance began. However, when interviewed, Chief Hilton vigorously denied the earlier report. In Peoria, 11 police officers were reportedly injured by shotgun blasts. However, Bernard J. Kennedy, Director of Public Safety, indicated that initial reports "were highly exaggerated" and that only seven officers were actually wounded. In East Point, Georgia, a white policeman had reportedly been injured during the disorder. Yet Acting Police Chief Hugh D. Brown indicated that there were no injuries to the police. In Little Rock, a policeman swore that he had been shot by a sniper. However, Chief of Police R. E. Brians told us that there was no injury and no broken skin. The Chief added that the policeman had been new and was not of the highest caliber. In fact, he is no longer with the department.

In addition, a closer look at the data reveals that the highest figures for numbers of policemen wounded by gunfire are misleading and need to be placed in perspective. Let us examine the three cases with the highest number of injuries: Cleveland with 10 policemen wounded by gunfire; Peoria, with seven; and Harvey-Dixmoor, Illinois, also with seven.

In Peoria, all seven policemen were wounded by the pellets from *a single shotgun blast*. In an interview, Safety

Director Kennedy stressed that "none of the injuries incurred were serious." The Harvey-Dixmoor incident was similar. There, five out of the seven injured were also hit by a single shotgun blast. Chief of Police Leroy H. Knapp Jr. informed us that only two or three shots were fired during the entire disorder. (A similar scattering of pellets occurred in St. Paul, where three out of four policemen hit by gunfire received their injuries from one shotgun blast.)

In Cleveland, almost every injury to a policeman came as a result of gunfire. However, it is not at all clear whether snipers inflicted the damage. In the chaos that accompanies many disorders, shots have sometimes been fired accidentally—by both rioters and policemen. Ripley's September 2 article in *The New York Times* stated the problem very well: "Only by setting the exact position of each man when he was shot, tracing the bullet paths, and locating all other policemen at the scene can a reasonable answer be found." Thus far, no information concerning the circumstances of each casualty in the Cleveland disorder has been disclosed, and this goes for deaths as well as injuries.

Moreover, what applies to Cleveland applies to the other disorders as well. The Little Rock case illustrates the point. Chief of Police Brians verified the shooting of a National Guardsman. However, he also clarified the circumstances of the shooting. He said that during the disorder a group of people gathered on a patio above a courtyard near the area where the National Guard was stationed. One individual, under the influence of alcohol, fired indiscriminantly into the crowd, hitting a guardsman in the foot. Chief Brians added: "He might just as easily have hit a [civil-rights] protestor as a guardsman." What is clear is that the circumstances concerning all casualties need to be clarified so as to avoid faulty inferences and incorrect judgments as much as possible.

Concerning the amount of sniping, there were numerous discrepancies between early and later reports, suggesting that many initial reports were exaggerated.

According to the police officials themselves, other than in the case of Cleveland where 25 to 30 snipers were allegedly involved, there were relatively few snipers. In 15 out of 17 cases where such information was available, police officials said there were three snipers or less. And in 7 out of 17 cases, the officials directly contradicted press reports at the time and said that no snipers were involved!

As for the number of gunshots fired by snipers, the reality, as reported by police, was again a lot less exciting than the newspapers indicated. In 15 out of 18 cases where information was available, "snipers" fired fewer than 10 shots. In 12 out of 18 cases, snipers fired fewer than five. Generally, then, in more than one-quarter of the cases in which sniping was originally reported, later indications were that no sniping had actually occurred.

In Evansville, initial reports indicated that a minimum of eight shots were fired. Yet Assistant Chief of Police Charles M. Gash told us that only one shot was fired.

A more dramatic illustration is found in the case of East Point, Georgia. Although 50 shots were reportedly fired at the time, Acting Chief of Police Hugh Brown informed us that no shots were fired.

In York, 11 persons were wounded in a "gun battle" on the first night. However, it turns out that 10 out of 11 persons were civilians and were injured by shotgun pellets. Only two snipers were involved, and only two to four shots were fired throughout the entire disturbance.

In Waterloo, Iowa, Chief of Police Robert S. Wright acknowledged that shots were fired, but he added: "We wouldn't consider it sniper fire." He told us that there was "no ambush, no concealment of participants, or anything like that." Moreover, he stated that not more than three persons out of a crowd of 50 youths carried weapons and "not a great number of shots were fired." The weapons used were small handguns.

In St. Paul, where 10 shots were reportedly fired at police and four officers were wounded by gunshots, Chief of Police Lester McAuliffe also acknowledged that though there was gunfire, there "wasn't any sniper fire as such."

A similar situation was found in Peoria. Safety Director Kennedy said that the three shots believed fired did not constitute actual sniping.

In Little Rock, Chief Brians discounted reports of widespread sniping and indicated that many "shots" were really firecrackers.

In Gary, early reports were that Chief of Police James Hilton had been fired upon and six persons had been wounded by snipers. Assistant Chief of Police Charles Boone told us that while a few shots might have been "fired in the air," no actual sniping occurred. No one was shot during the disturbance, and no one was injured. Chief Hilton indicated that the fireman who was supposed to have been hit during the outbreak was actually shot by a drunk *prior* to the disorder.

In a few instances, discrepancies between first reports and sober reappraisal can be traced to exaggerations of the policemen themselves. However, most of the discrepancies already cited throughout this report can be attributed to the press—at both the local and national level. In some instances, the early press reports (those appearing at the time of the incident) were so inexplicit as to give the *impression* of a great deal of sniping. In other instances, the early figures given were simply exaggerated. In still other instances, the early reports failed to distinguish between sniper fire and other forms of gunplay.

Moreover, the press generally gave far too little attention to the immediate cause or causes of the disturbance. Even in the aftermath of the violence, few attempts were made to verify previous statements or to survey the tensions and grievances rooted in the community. Instead, newspapers in many instances placed an unusually heavy (and at times distorted) emphasis on the most dramatic aspects of the violence, particularly where sniping was concerned.

A look at some of the newspaper headlines during the disorders is most revealing, especially where the "pellet cases" are involved. As mentioned earlier, large numbers of casualties were sustained from the pellets of a single shotgun blast—in Peoria, seven policemen; in Harvey-Dixmoor, five policemen, and in York, 10 civilians were injured in this way; the most commonly cited examples of a "new pattern" of violence. Unfortunately, inaccurate and sensational headlines created an impression of widespread sniping, with the police singled out as the principal targets. A few individual acts of violence were so enlarged as to convey to the reader a series of "bloodbaths." In some cases, an explanation of the circumstances surrounding the injuries was buried in the news story. In other cases, no explanation was given. In still other cases, the number of casualties was exaggerated.

Distorted headlines were found in the local press:

RACE VIOLENCE ERUPTS: DOZEN SHOT IN PEORIA
Chicago (Ill.) *Tribune,*
July 31, 1968
6 COPS ARE SHOT IN HARVEY STRIFE
Chicago *Sun-Times,*
August 7, 1968

20 HURT AS NEW VIOLENCE RAKES WEST END AREA
11 FELLED BY GUN FIRE, FOUR FIREMEN INJURED FIGHTING FIVE BLAZES

York (Pa.) *Dispatch,*
August 5, 1968

These distortions were transmitted on the wire services as well. For example, in Ann Arbor, Michigan, readers were given the following accounts of Peoria and Harvey-Dixmoor in their local newspapers. The first account was based up-on a United Press International news dispatch; the second is from an Associated Press dispatch.

10 POLICEMEN SHOT IN PEORIA VIOLENCE
By United Press International
Ann Arbor (Mich.) *News,*
July 30, 1968

Ten policemen were wounded by shotgun blasts today during a four-hour flareup of violence in Peoria, Ill. . . .

EIGHT WOUNDED IN CHICAGO AREA

Ann Arbor *News,*
August 7, 1968

Harvey, Ill. (AP)—Sporadic gunfire wounded seven policemen and a woman during a disturbance caused by Negro youths, and scores of law enforcement officers moved in early today to secure the troubled area. . . .

Finally, they were repeated in headlines and stories appearing in the national press:

GUNFIRE HITS 11 POLICEMEN IN ILL. VIOLENCE

Washington Post,
July 31, 1968

SHOTGUN ASSAULTS IN PEORIA GHETTO WOUND 9 POLICEMEN

The Law Officer,
Fall, 1968

Chicago—On August 6, in the suburbs of Harvey and Dixmoor, seven policemen and a woman were shot in Negro disturbances which a Cook County undersheriff said bore signs of having been planned.

U.S. News & World Report
August 19, 1968

In all probability, few newspapers or reporters could withstand this type of criticism. Nevertheless, it does seem that the national press bears a special responsibility. Few of the nationally known newspapers and magazines attempted to verify sniping reports coming out of the cities; few were willing to undertake independent investigations of their own; and far too many were overly zealous in their reports of a "trend" based on limited and unconfirmed evidence. Stated very simply: The national press overreacted.

For some time now, many observers (including members of the academic community) have been predicting a change from spontaneous to premeditated outbreaks resembling guerrilla warfare. Their predictions have largely been based upon limited evidence such as unconfirmed reports of arms caches and the defiant, sometimes revolutionary rhetoric of militants.

And then came Cleveland. At the time, the July disorder in that city appeared to fulfill all the predictions—intelligence reports of planning prior to the disorder, intensive sniping directed at the police, the absence of a precipitating incident, and so on. Few people at the time quarreled with the appraisal in *The New York Times* that Cleveland was "perhaps the first documented case" of a planned uprising against the police. Following the events in Cleveland, disorders in which shots may have been fired were immediately suspected to be part of a "wave."

Unwittingly or not, the press has been constructing a scenario on armed uprisings. The story line of this scenario is not totally removed from reality. There *have* been a few shoot-outs with the police, and a handful may have been planned. But no wave of uprisings and no set pattern of murderous conflict have developed—at least not yet. Has the press provided the script for future conspiracies? Why hasn't the scenario been acted out until now? The answers to these questions are by no means certain. What is clear is that the press has critical responsibilities in this area.

for any act of violence easily attracts the attention of the vicarious viewer as well as the participant.

Moreover, in an era when most Americans are informed by radio and television, the press should place far greater emphasis on interpreting, rather than merely reporting, the news. Background pieces on the precipitating events and tension-heightening incidents, more detailed information on the sniper himself, and investigations concerning police and civilian casualties represent fertile areas for the news analyst. To close, here is one concrete example: While four policemen were killed in the violence reviewed in this article, at least 16 civilians were also killed. A report on the circumstances of these deaths might provide some important insights into the disorders.

July/August 1969

FURTHER READING SUGGESTED BY THE AUTHOR:

The Paranoid Style in American Politics and Other Essays by Richard Hofstadter (New York: Knopf, 1966). A historian looks at the receptiveness of Americans to conspiratorial theories.

Shoot-out in Cleveland; Black Militants and the Police: July 23, 1968. A report of the Civil Violence Research Center by Louis H. Masotti and James J. Corsi (Cleveland, Ohio: Case Western Reserve University, submitted to the National Commission on the Causes and Prevention of Violence, May 16, 1969). This is an indepth account of the background, nature, and circumstances of the July, 1968 disorder.

Public Information and Civil Disorders, National League of Cities, Department of Urban Studies (Washington, D.C.: July, 1968) contains recommendations concerning the activities of the news media during civil disorders.

Report of the National Advisory Commission on Civil Disorders (Washington, D.C.: Government Publishing Office, 1968). Chapter 15 evaluates the media coverage of civil disorders during the Summer of 1967.

No Heaven for Hell's Angels

ROBERT SHELLOW/DEREK V. ROEMER

Ever since Marlon Brando portrayed the leather-jacketed leader of a motorcycle gang in "The Wild Ones," a squadron of free-wheeling, anti-social highway roamers has loomed as a symbol of menace to many small communities across the country. In recent summers major riots have broken out at resort towns when unruly crowds have disrupted a schedule of motorcycle races and forced the police or National Guard into action.

As social scientists and police consultants we became involved in the summer of 1965 in a motorcycle riot that never happened. The experience we shared with a police department may be instructive in coping with riot conditions that confront communities in the future, not only with motorcycle gangs, but in the public arena of social protest.

A national motorcycle race was scheduled for Labor Day weekend at Upper Marlboro, the county seat of Prince George's County, Maryland. The county, with a population of 500,000, is adjacent to Washington, D.C., and is partly suburban, partly rural. Upper Marlboro is a rural sector, but is only about 15 miles from well-populated suburbs.

The news media had reported all the gory details of the Weir's Beach riot on the Fourth of July which followed the National Championship motorcycle race near Laconia, New Hampshire. A police lieutenant reported that shortly after the Weir's Beach episode three motorcyclists, proclaiming themselves members of the notorious "Hell's Angels" of California, were arrested and jailed for disorderly conduct by town policemen in Prince George's County. Angered by being forced to bathe for a court appearance, they threatened to return over Labor Day to "tear up the county."

Learning of these events in a casual conversation with the lieutenant, and wishing to keep posted on the local situation, we spoke to the police inspector responsible for police action over Labor Day. He wasn't sure how seriously he ought to take these threats and rumors. Precious little was known about the Hell's Angels and how they were likely to behave among several thousand motorcyclists amassed for a big race. We offered to chase down the rumors, and bring the results of our inquiries back to the police. But two weeks of search failed to turn up so much as one Hell's Angel, though the rumors of invasion and destruction were persistent and proliferating.

When we reviewed accounts of several recent riots and disturbances in connection with recreational or sporting events, we noted several common factors that seemed significant in all of them:

■ An influx of outsiders into a small town or circumscribed amusement area, where the number of outsiders was large relative to the number of local inhabitants and police.

■ The outsiders were distinguished from "locals" by some common feature—an intense interest (such as motorcycling), an age group (college youth), race, etc.

■ The distinction between "locals" and "outsiders" was often made more visible by differences in dress, argot, and other expressive behavior.

The specific conditions under which exuberance and rowdiness exploded into rioting seemed to be the following:

■ Recreational, service, and control facilities were "flooded" by overwhelming numbers of visitors who were left at loose ends. They were ready for any kind of "action."

■ Ineffectual, often provocative attempts at control and expression of authority were made by police or civic officials.

■ A sense of group solidarity developed among members of the crowd.

Often the locals, including the authorities, contributed to the developing cohesion of outsiders by viewing the visitors as all of a kind; attributing negative class characteristics to them (dirty, rowdy, etc.) ; labelling them as "hoodlums" or "young punks"; and then treating them accordingly. The effect of opposition or attack in solidifying group cohesion is well documented. If the opposition is ineffectual as well, many members of the developing mob begin to sense their own potential power. (Several reports mentioned careful preplanning by a small cadre of dedicated instigators, who allegedly circulated rumors before the event and selected targets on the scene. Actual proof of "planning," as opposed to repetition of rumors, is difficult to obtain.)

In order to prepare for the special Labor Day situation ahead, we needed information about the organization of motorcycling both as a sport and as a way of life. Moving from one enthusiast to another, and interviewing at the local Harley-Davidson dealer, we made a number of discoveries. Motorcyclists come from all walks of life. The majority are employed, and need to be, since as much as $3,000 may be tied up in a "motor." The devotees insist that the size of the machine separates the men from the boys. Those who own enormous Harley-Davidsons and the large Triumphs or BSA's and who engage in competitive events such as races, "field events," and "hill climbs," see themselves as a breed apart from the "candy ass" owners of Hondas and the lightweights. For the former group, the motorcycle often serves as the fulcrum of social and even family life. They enjoy being able to take off any evening at a moment's notice and ride, say from Washington, D.C., to Atlantic City, returning as the sun rises. They travel regularly to field meets and races, usually camping overnight on the scene.

Like many hobby-sports, motorcycling has its formal organization, the American Motorcycle Association (AMA), and its "sanctioned" members. AMA clubs have tight rules and tolerate little deviance. Some non-AMA clubs are similar and may aspire to sanctioned status. Other clubs are available to those who enjoy a more relaxed and casual organization; these may require only that members not seriously embarrass the club in public. They tend to be more tolerant in their attitudes regarding noisy mufflers and styling, and less regimented during group expeditions. All get classified by the AMA as "outlaws."

Aside from these more or less conforming clubs, the "outlaw" class also includes groups of dedicated rowdies who pride themselves on their ability to intimidate and destroy. The Hell's Angels Motorcycle Club of California is such a group, as are the Gooses, from New York and New Jersey, or the Pagans, from the Washington area.

Spokesmen for the motorcycling "establishment" often attribute the sport's bad image to the "1 percent who cause all the trouble." The rowdies have proudly accepted "1-percenter" as an honorific epithet, and often have it emblazoned on their costume as a badge of commitment. The

1-percenter personifies the motorcycle hoodlum stereotype.

Regardless of their organization or status within the sport, motorcyclists agree on one thing—they all complain of police persecution. They also report being victimized on the roads by car drivers. Many respectable motorcyclists sympathize with the view the "rowdy outlaws" have of themselves as a persecuted minority.

With regard to the Labor Day weekend itself, we learned that the schedule of events was more complex than we or the police had thought. Aside from the big race on Sunday, the "Ninth Annual Tobacco Trail Classic" (for the first time a National Championship event) at the Upper Marlboro track, there were lesser races at the same track on Saturday. At the Vista track, 14 miles away but within the same police jurisdiction, there were to be "field events" such as drag races and "riding the plank" on Saturday and Sunday and an AMA-sanctioned race meet on Monday. The sponsors of the Upper Marlboro races had also scheduled a Saturday night race at a track 30 miles away in the Baltimore suburbs, "to give people something to do and keep them out of trouble."

The Vista track had in the past operated as an "outlaw" track without AMA sanction, and most or all of the competitors and spectators had been Negroes. However, in 1965 it had just achieved sanctioned status, and its events were listed in the national calendar. A dance hall, popular with Washington area Negroes, was located in the track infield and would be operating every night of the weekend, so it appeared that a large proportion of those attending the motorcycle events at Vista would be Negroes. The crowd at the Marlboro track was expected to be between 3,000 and 6,000; a much smaller croud was expected at Vista. Most motorcyclists we spoke to thought there would be a great deal of migration during the weekend from one track to another and among the various camping areas (assuming there were more than one), the taverns, and other recreation spots. Easy mobility is the essence of motorcycling.

Concluding that we enjoyed a special and privileged relationship with motorcyclists, the police asked us whether or not the race should be called off. We did not feel justified in taking responsibility for the decision, but joined in the deliberations. To cancel a public event on the basis of thin rumor alone—the Hell's Angels threat—was a dangerous precedent to set, yet to jeopardize the safety of innocent people was unthinkable. The police decided to permit the race as scheduled, while making every effort to avert violence. (Our shift in role from outside consultant to partnership with the police at this point tied us much closer to the action and events of the weekend than would ordinarily be the case in the role of scientist-observer.)

Once the decision to permit the race was made, we developed a set of goals which we felt should guide planning, basing our thinking on the analysis of recent riots mentioned above and on a hurried and therefore unsystematic study of the social science literature. *Collective Behavior,* by Ralph Turner and Lewis Killian (1957) was particularly useful and supported our inferences from the riot accounts.

First, we encouraged sober planning for all the events of the long weekend. Naturally, advance planning was not new to the police department. Nonetheless we were grateful that the unsettled state of the "Hell's Angels" rumors, plus our refusal to make pseudo-authoritative pronouncements on the probable course of events, helped maintain some controlled anxiety among police officials. This limited anxiety went far to prevent a premature resolution of the planning process, either through panicky reliance on harshness on the one hand, or complacent relaxation on the other. Our goal was a plan with three major objectives:

■ anticipation of the kinds, numbers, and distribution of motorcyclists and spectators; the activities they would engage in; and the amount of localized roving to be expected;

■ the disposition of police officers and their instructions, both as to general attitude and specific actions to meet various contingencies;

■ coordination of the several police departments concerned, including the state police, and the local police of nearby towns and counties to which the motorcyclists might travel in search of recreation.

Our second goal was to avoid a polarization of relations between the authorities and the motorcyclists. We directed our efforts to both groups. As we explored the "culture" of motorcycling, we tried to keep the police informed and interested in what we learned. We arranged a meeting between some local motorcyclists and police officials at which films of sport motorcycling were shown; afterward each group expressed its gripes concerning the other. Our educational goals with the police were:

■ to show that motorcyclists are not essentially different from other citizens, and need not be treated as a breed apart;

■ to inform them that in point of fact motorcyclists are not a homogeneous class but come in a variety of shapes and sizes, some innocuous, some potentially troublesome;

■ to impress upon them that indiscriminate harsh treatment of all motorcyclists would confirm the latter's sense of persecution, increase group solidarity among them, and go far toward creating the very polarization we wished to avoid.

In working with local motorcyclists, our objectives were:

■ to involve the organized groups in the control effort, asking them not only to refrain from participating in or serving as passive audience to rowdiness, but to help actively in identifying potential trouble areas and keeping police informed of large group movements;

■ to weaken the respectable motorcyclists' sense of solidarity with the "1-percenters" by reinforcing their concern for the deteriorating "image" of motorcycling and pointing out their vested interest in running peaceful races.

Our third major goal was to ensure that adequate facilities were provided for the visiting motorcyclists, with an eye to both containment and entertainment. Our objective was to inhibit the milling behavior that usually precedes crowd disturbances. Specifically, we suggested that adequate and convenient camping facilities were customary and essential at motorcycle meets. Also certain informal and rather dangerous recreations (such as drag racing and stunt riding in the camp grounds), which do not impinge on the non-motorcycling citizenry, are also customary and ought to be permitted. We had noted in the New Hampshire riots that the only camping area was 40 to 50 miles from the track. The campers were reluctant to make the long return trip after each day's racing, and some preferred simply to stay up all night. Thus they remained in the town of Weir's Beach long past the time when they might ordinarily have returned to secluded camping areas for an evening of dragracing, motor-revving and beer drinking—in mutually acceptable segregation from the resort citizenry.

Our fourth major objective was to monitor the events of the weekend and keep a continuous flow of intelligence coming into police command headquarters, so that the senior officer could make effective decisions. Here we served in something of a combined research and undercover capacity, checking out rumors, keeping current with the temper of various groups, clubs, and gangs among the motorcyclists, and observing fights or accidents as they occurred. We made a point of spending time in places where the county police could not routinely go.

Rumors of the arrival *en masse* of the Hell's Angels of California persisted through Saturday of the three-day weekend and were *never* clearly proved or disproved. We learned that Hell's Angels were anticipated in resorts all the way from Ocean City, Maryland, 140 miles away, to the Pacific coast. Rumors circulated mostly among youth and motorcyclists that three scattered locations (a tavern, the race track, and a whole town) in Prince George's County were to be wrecked. We began to see that the Hell's Angels were assuming a mythical character. They had become folk heroes—vicarious exemplars of behavior most youth could only fantasy (unless swept away in mob activity), and legendary champions who would come to the rescue of the oppressed and persecuted. An older motorcyclist, witnessing police harassment of his fellows at a town outside Prince George's County, was heard to remark, "Just wait 'til the Angels hear about this when they come in tomorrow. They'll come tear this place apart."

The police never did accept the idea of actively involving local motorcycle clubs in the control effort, even though we offered to do all the leg work in getting club representatives together for a meeting. An exception was the large club that sponsored the Marlboro races. The inspector warned them severely that any trouble this weekend would greatly reduce the likelihood of the race being permitted next year. However, he emphasized that the department did not intend to discriminate in any way against motorcyclists. The inspector convinced the sponsoring club to hire uniformed guards for the race track. The club also assured us that camping facilities would be provided.

There was little advance coordination among the various police departments in the area. The state police announced a policy of "keep them moving," and said they would "get tough" with any rowdy-looking types they encountered. The detailed cooperation between departments we had envisioned, like involvement of the motorcycle clubs in police planning, was probably considered too far outside normal practice to be warranted by the situation.

Despite these largely negative circumstances, one particularly positive development stood out. At each police roll call prior to the Labor Day weekend, all the uniformed men were instructed to treat motorcyclists just as they would any motorist visiting the county. They were told that only a very small minority of motorcyclists were troublemakers, and that only the behavior, not the style of dress, haircut, or bodily cleanliness was a matter of police concern.

On Saturday morning of the race weekend, we and the police were dismayed to learn that the sponsoring AMA club had reneged on its promise to provide public camping facilities. Apparently they wished to avoid the expense of renting portable outhouses, which were likely to be broken up for firewood in the course of the weekend. We were further disturbed to learn that early arrivals, some of whom were pretty ragged and rough looking, had already set up a squatters' camp in the large field usually rented for that purpose.

This created a tricky problem for the police. They could not legitimately enter the field, which was private property, unless the owner complained or a violation of law occurred which was visible from the public highway. If the police officially notified the owner, he would be bound to ask that the trespassers be removed, because of his liability for damages incurred by people who were on his property with his implicit permission. Eviction of the growing crowd of squatters would have meant removing a noisy, potentially·

troublesome group from a location remote from residences and businesses where the amount of property they could damage was limited. Furthermore, they were not, at that time, visibly violating laws. There was no way to predict where they would go if evicted, but obviously they would not go home so early in the weekend. The problem might simply have been scattered all over the county, aggravating the difficulties of control while at the same time provoking resentment, which could have been turned against innocent citizens.

It was decided that notification of the owner of the field was not warranted and that there were tactical advantages in keeping the field open, since it seemed to be attracting and holding the rowdier element. So long as they were all in one place, surveillance would be simple and response to trouble could be quick.

The activities on the field were kept under continuous but unobtrusive observation. Police cars were continually passing the field, occasionally pausing near the entrance; the people on the field were thus kept aware of the police presence in the general area, but not so heavily as to arouse feelings of persecution. The 45-man Civil Disturbance Unit (CDU), trained in riot control but lacking experience in full riot conditions, had been mobilized and sent out on the road the night before (Friday). Only a few motorcyclists were seen in the county and the CDU was dismissed around midnight. The usual dance at the Vista track was held without incident.

From Saturday through Monday the entire force, including the CDU, was ordered on 12-hour shifts. The men were kept on the road except when responding to trouble calls, thus providing extra control for the normally heavy holiday beach traffic. We felt that the men would be able to respond more quickly to large-scale trouble if they had been concentrated in two or three central standby locations rather than dispersed over the county's 486 square miles. However, police officials judged that the disadvantage of a possible delay in such emergency mobilization was offset by the double payoff from the same investment in overtime pay—more extensive traffic control *and* riot prevention.

An elaborate communications system was set up, employing not only the police radio (monitored by newspapers and wire services) but also a civil defense band, which permitted more detailed discussion and open references to likely trouble spots. This privacy greatly facilitated unobtrusive surveillance. A special radio code was established so that squad cars using the police band could notify headquarters briefly and in confidence of the presence of groups of motorcyclists.

On Saturday, only a few hundred spectators attended the scheduled lightweight and novice races at Marlboro. Across the highway those squatters, dusty out-of-towners, and locals who preferred the role of contestant to that of passive onlooker conducted their own impromptu field games. The entire center of the squatters' field, despite its ruts and hummocks, became a drag strip. Groups, clubs, even families had set up camp sites around the periphery of the field in a broken crescent.

Groups and couples who settled on the extreme ends of the crescent appeared to have expensive camping equipment and rather conventional dress. Dead center at the head of the drag strip, the most ragged troop of squatters set up headquarters in a large army tent, its center pole flying a red flag. Sullen young men and girls milled around this command post drinking beer and making menacing noises at curiosity seekers. Clusters of jackets marked "Hell's

Angels," "Pagans," or "The Gooses," were seen. Some individuals sported a nose ring, a swastika, a Halloween wig, or gold cross earrings; many men wore their hair in shoulder-length manes.

A group of mostly short-haired locals, more or less neat in T-shirts and jeans, tried to introduce some order into the drag races. One tried to control racing by flagging each pair of racers to a start. He was successful for several hours but finally the enormous quantities of beer, hard liquor, and green wine consumed by participants undermined the authority he had established. Racers roared past him without waiting for the flag. He shouted for order, but few responded. Non-racers crisscrossed the drag strip, narrowly escaping collision.

The proximity of the self-appointed track superintendents to the encampment of rowdy long-haired outsiders and locals became abrasive. Accidents began to occur. Finally a fight broke out between a very wobbly Pagan and a helmeted, short-haired local. After punching the Pagan unconscious, the short-haired hero was successfully defended by his associates from being pummelled by the rest of the Pagans. The victor had the poor taste and bad judgment to sit triumphantly astride the hood of a truck, waving his beer can in a bravado challenge for all to see. Now all the rowdy groups joined in a confederation and charged *en masse* toward the short-haired locals. Just at that moment a drunken cyclist lost his machine to a rut in the track. His mishap was noted by police on the highway who dispatched an ambulance along with five police cruisers. The vehicles poured onto the field and fanned out in a half-circle around the casualty, thus coincidentally presenting the crowd with an array of flashing red lights. The unexpected show of power was so sudden and instantaneous that the would-be warriors at the head of the strip broke ranks and returned to their staging area. Unknowingly the police had put a stop to what might have been a bloody war, since the local motorcycle enthusiasts were far outnumbered by the combined force of Pagans, "Hell's Angels," and Gooses. (We put "Hell's Angels" in quotes wherever the reference is to participants in local events, because we have serious doubts that any *bona fide* members were ever present in our area.)

Following the withdrawal of police, 20 "Hell's Angels" and Gooses set out to replenish their beer supply at the Old Tavern nearby. Just as they started to throw their weight around in the bar and threaten the owner, a police sergeant and another officer entered the room. The group quieted down and waited for the action. Three cyclists moved to the window to assess the size of the sergeant's force; four cruisers were visible. The sergeant opened with, "I hope you all are behaving yourselves." He remembered from a conversation with us that motorcycle chains worn loosely over the hips rather than through belt loops should be considered weapons, so he asked, "What's that chain for?" "Hey, man, I lock up my motor with it." "Well, aren't you afraid someone'll steal your motor, not being locked up and all? You better come with me while we put that chain on right, son." The group tensed, then relaxed as the young man elected to go quietly and do as the sergeant suggested. Shortly after this low-key encounter the group roared back to the field and the Old Tavern was prematurely closed for the weekend.

At 11 p.m. about 75 cyclists were seen by one of our staff at a rock 'n roll beach resort in a neighboring county. The chief of police there had already advised the press of his intention to lock up any rowdy motorcyclists who showed up. He arranged for the state police to back him up. Twenty state troopers in riot dress and five dogs were lined up on the main street across from the crowd of motorcycle riders while six local policemen pushed and poked with night sticks, arresting several who took exception to their tactics. By 1:30 Sunday morning most of the motorcyclists had left town. Statements to the press by the chief greatly exaggerated the numbers present and arrested, thus giving an unwarranted notoriety to the evening.

By Sunday morning 300 motorcyclists had settled on the field at Marlboro. Those who had been driven from the beach resort were in a mean mood. Under the direction of the unofficial starter drag racing resumed at a more frantic tempo than on the day before. Across the highway a steady stream of spectators poured onto the track for the afternoon race. Few took notice of the accidents that were beginning to occur on the field.

At 2 p.m. a fire was set in a railroad caboose on a siding behind the field. Fire equipment and police responded quickly; no attempt was made to find the arsonists. At 3 p.m. a crane was started on an adjacent construction site and tools were stolen from its cab. At 4:30, coinciding with the "Tobacco Trail Classic" across the road, a man removed the license plates from his dilapidated old car and set it afire. With another sportsman straddling the hood, the owner drove onto the drag strip and jumped free. The car rammed an accelerating motorcycle. Both hood rider and motorcyclist were thrown on impact, both suffering broken legs. A fire truck arrived to put out the fire amid jeers from spectators. A police lieutenant supervised aid to the injured, making humorous asides to cool the excited crowd and enable the ambulance to remove the casualties to the hospital.

About 6 p.m. the long-haired groups demanded that locals turn over the starting flag to a "Hell's Angel" who appeared to be one of their leaders. Fighting broke out but subsided immediately when one squad of the CDU (10 men) drove onto the field. This time the police had riot equipment visible—helmets, clubs, shotguns, gas masks. The crowd dispersed; the squad withdrew. Since tension on the field seemed to be building, command officers set up an observation post on a cloverleaf approach overlooking the field. At 6:30 the flagman and a delegation from his club came up to plead with command officers to clear the field of hoodlums; they threatened to bring in their own weapons if police didn't protect them. Since the delegation could not agree on who should be charged with what, action was delayed.

At 7 p.m. several men broke away from the milling crowd at the center of the field and ran to their machines. From the observation post, it was clear they were returning with bars, chains, and other weapons. The entire CDU was sent on to the field where they quickly assembled in riot formation. The inspector drawled out over the bull-horn, "All right men, you've had your fun, now it's time to go home." Before he finished his sentence motorcycles began to move out of the field. Within 20 minutes the area was clear.

Up to this time, the importance of containing trouble makers on the field was dominant in the minds of commanding officers. But if the crowd were allowed to remain overnight, fighting probably would continue, under the cover of darkness. Dispersing all the squatters while it was still light would, hopefully, send them on their way home. The alternative—isolating and removing the instigators and mob leaders—was complicated because the police could not remain on the field and because cyclists were unable or unwilling to serve as complainants.

Fifteen minutes after the field was vacated, 10 men and a girl were arrested outside the Old Tavern, where they had started to break windows. Within minutes, another 10, including the leading "Hell's Angel," were arrested as trespassers at a filling station where they refused to make way for customers. There was no further trouble in the county, at the Vista track, or at the beach resort, though an anxious lookout was maintained until early the next morning. By Monday it was obvious that the danger had passed.

Both the command officers and the county commissioner responsible for police matters were satisfied that the police had conducted themselves effectively and that the control effort had been a success. They felt, however, that the situation had not warranted the extra expense and trouble. Estimates of cost ranged from $6,000 to $10,000, but certainly some of the overtime pay would have been necessary for a Labor Day weekend even without motorcyclists. The commissioner announced that he couldn't see why the county had "to put up with the influx of motorcycle tramps who camp out, drink and fight among themselves."

Like the commissioner, most of the police leadership was opposed to permitting the race next year. We refrained from offering unsolicited and premature advice on the issue of future races. The club sponsoring the Marlboro races was considering cutting the meet down to a one-day event and preventing camping altogether, in the hope that this would make the event more acceptable to authorities.

Since we were unable to maintain contact among Pagans, Gooses, or "Hell's Angels," we could not ascertain their reactions to police policy and procedure. We did talk to our acquaintance at the local Harley-Davidson dealership, which provides service and parts for many out-of-town motorcycles. He reported that for the first time in nine years of races he had heard none of the usual atrocity stories of police mistreatment of motorcyclists. The local short-haired motorcyclists who had been in the fighting on the field felt that police had exercised entirely too much restraint in dealing with that situation. They did not know, until we told them, that the field had not been rented this year.

Was all the concern, planning, and extra police activity justified? We think so. Would the Gooses, Pagans and alleged "Hell's Angels" have been just as peaceful anyway, despite their frightening appearance? We think not. Consider the forays against the Old Tavern, the crane, and the caboose, the incinerated car, and the brawling which broke out repeatedly on the field. If unhindered and undaunted, the hoodlum element sooner or later would have left the camping area and sought glory and reputation in new arenas, before new audiences. These seem to be people who need and seek the stimulation of collective action, excitement, and violence. Without it they become depressed and demoralized. They have an affinity for the romantic role of outlaw, which is perhaps the only status in which they feel they can stand out as individuals.

Four factors were critical in preventing the spread of violence:

■ Most important was the general police policy of strength, fairness, and neutrality, which influenced all the tactics employed. Law violations were dealt with immediately and firmly, but motorcyclists were not harassed or deliberately antagonized. The availability of overwhelming force, literally on a moment's notice, was demonstrated but not overdramatized. Thus potential mob leaders were deprived of the rallying point of "police brutality," and potential followers never developed the sense of mob power that results from evidence of police weakness.

■ The decision not to interfere with the motorcyclists who camped and drag raced on private property, until extreme violence impended, was also of critical importance, for several reasons. In the field the potential troublemakers were all contained in an open area where all their activities could be easily observed. They were segregated by the broad highway and differentiated from the much larger mass of spectators at the track, and thus deprived of both victims and audience. The amount of property vulnerable to damage was relatively small. Finally, they were allowed to occupy their time with activities which were both customary and satisfying (drinking, dragging, showing off, etc.) while not annoying other citizens. This business of "keeping them occupied" is not trivial. Mob action, except in a catastrophe, is usually preceded by a period of "milling," exchange of fact and rumor, and movement toward consensus. During such periods mob leaders can seize the initiative in directing the crowd toward specific objectives.

■ Another important factor was the continuous flow of intelligence both during the weekend and over the preceding weeks, important for helping break down police stereotypes as well as for its operational utility.

■ Plain and simple good luck favored us on several occasions. Undoubtedly there was an element of luck in the fact that the "hoodlum element" chose to remain at the campground rather than roam the county. The factional dispute between the short-haired locals and the "1-percenters" may have been fortunate in that it kept the warlike elements busy and precluded any alliance between the two groups. It was especially fortunate that when it finally became necessary to clear the field, most of the rowdier motorcyclists left the county entirely.

As it turned out we successfully avoided a general polarization of motorcyclists against police and the citizenry. We tried to apply in this situation the specialized knowledge and theory of our field, and found it useful. The police, logically, focus on the apprehension of persons who violate laws, protection of citizens from the acts of such persons, prevention of specifically violative behavior, and the deployment of strength in accordance with those goals. As social scientists we focused on the collection of data, the analysis of differences and similarities, the understanding of group and individual behavior, and the communication and exchange of fact and opinion. (The clarity with which these distinctions are drawn is not meant to deny that there are policemen who think like social scientists, and *vice versa*.)

Though the events of Labor Day, 1965, in Prince George's County were of little national or long-term import in themselves, we consider the principles applied and the lessons learned to have far broader relevance—a significant practice for things to come.

July/August 1966

NOTES ON CONTRIBUTORS

Philip Ennis   "Crime, Victims and Police"

Professor of sociology at Wesleyan University, Middletown, Connecticut. Ennis was formerly Senior Study Director at the National Opinion Research Center, University of Chicago, and director of a study on criminal victimization for the President's Crime Commission.

Terry Ann Knopf   "Sniping—a New Pattern of Violence?"

Research associate at the Lemberg Center for the Study of Violence at Brandeis University. Knopf has authored *Youth Patrols: An Experiment in Community Participation* and has written several articles on press coverage of racial disorders.

Tom Parmenter   "Breakdown in Law and Order"

Editor of *Inequality in Education*, the bulletin of the Harvard Center for Law and Education. Parmenter wrote this article while a Russel Sage Fellow at *trans*action magazine. He is a former reporter for *Chicago's American* (now *Chicago Today*).

Albert J. Reiss, Jr.   "Police Brutality—Answers to Key Questions"

Professor of sociology at the University of Michigan and chairman of the department. Reiss has served on the President's Commission of Law Enforcement and Administration of Justice, 1966-67, and the National Advisory Commission on Civil Disorder, 1967-68, and has published books and articles on deviant behavior.

Derek V. Roemer   "No Heaven for Hell's Angels"

Psychologist, and has served with the National Institute of Mental Health. Roemer's interests include peer group formation in adolescents, which he studied in Washington, D.C.

Robert Shellow   "No Heaven for 'Hell's Angels'"

Chief of the National Institute of Mental Health's Adolescent Process Section and a former special advisor to the Department of Justice on police-community relations.